WINDERMERE

THE JEWEL OF LAKE ROSSEAU

WINDERMERE

THE JEWEL OF LAKE ROSSEAU

RICHARD TATLEY

The BOSTON MILLS PRESS

Published in 1999 by
BOSTON MILLS PRESS
132 Main Street
Erin, Ontario N0B 1T0
Tel 519-833-2407
Fax 519-833-2195
e-mail books@boston-mills.on.ca
www.boston-mills.on.ca

An affiliate of
STODDART PUBLISHING CO. LIMITED
34 Lesmill Road
Toronto, Ontario, Canada
M3B 2T6
Tel 416-445-3333
Fax 416-445-5967
e-mail gdsinc@genpub.com

Distributed in Canada by
General Distribution Services Limited
325 Humber College Boulevard
Toronto, Canada M9W 7C3
Orders 1-800-387-0141 Ontario & Quebec
Orders 1-800-387-0172 NW Ontario & Other Provinces
e-mail customer.service@ccmailgw.genpub.com
EDI Canadian Telebook S1150391

Distributed in the United States by
General Distribution Services Inc.
85 River Rock Drive, Suite 202
Buffalo, New York 14207-2170
Toll-free 1-800-805-1083
Toll-free fax 1-800-481-6207
e-mail gdsinc@genpub.com
www.genpub.com

03 02 01 00 99 1 2 3 4 5

Cataloguing in Publication Data
Tatley, Richard
Windermere
Includes bibliographical references.
ISBN 1-55046-235-0
1. Windermere House (Windermere, Ont.) – History. 2. Windermere (Ont.) – History.
I. Title.
FC3099.W5557T37 1998 971.3'16 C98-931132-5
F1059.W48T37 1998

Design by Mary Firth

Printed in Canada

PAGE 3: WINDERMERE HOUSE, CA. 1909. (FLORENCE AITKEN)

PAGE 5: VIEW FROM BALCONY, WINDERMERE HOUSE, LAKE ROSSEAU. (MICKLETHWAITE, NATIONAL ARCHIVES OF CANADA PA163205)

CONTENTS

Introduction 7

Chapter 1: The Early Days (1860–1896) 9

Chapter 2: The Glorious Years (1896–1929) 29

Chapter 3: The Difficult Years (1930–1970) 43

Chapter 4: Recent Years (1970–1997) 57

Chapter 5: Conclusion 66

Bibliography 67

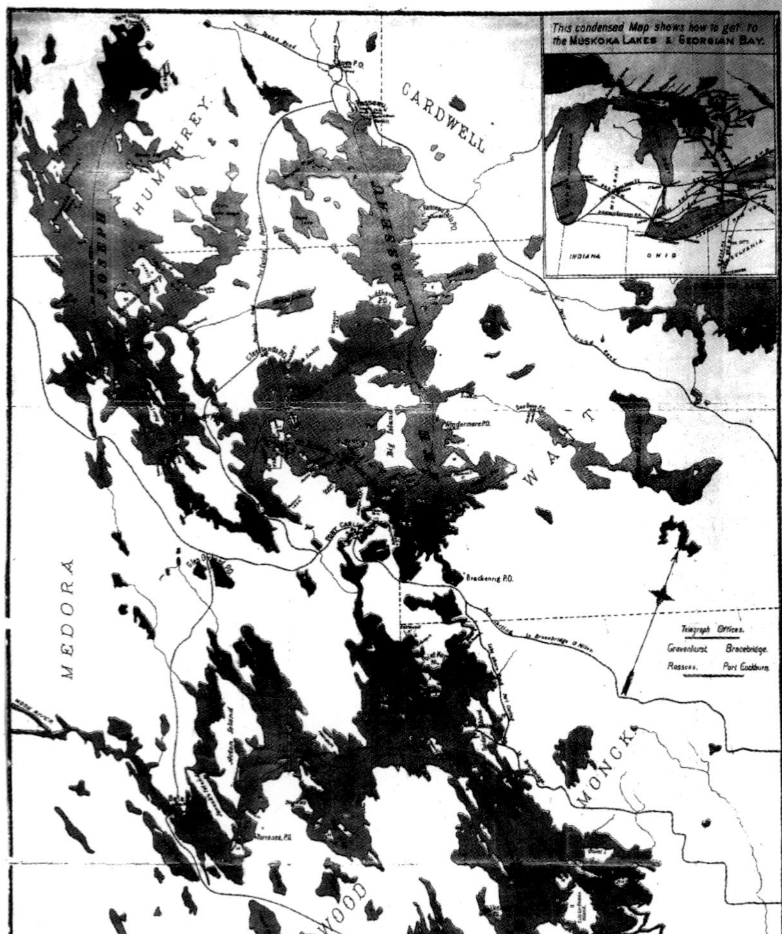

MAP OF WATT TOWNSHIP, 1878.

INTRODUCTION

THE VILLAGE OF WINDERMERE, ONTARIO, is a tiny community of about sixty households, nestled away in the Muskoka District, on the eastern shores of Lake Rosseau. It is a quiet little place, with barely 110 permanent inhabitants, located at the end of a dead-end road in the Township of Muskoka Lakes. To town planners and bureaucrats it is only a minor service centre for the adjacent area. Officially speaking, it does not even exist, except as a local post office. Upon arrival, one finds a single store, a former schoolhouse turned community centre, two charming churches, a small wharf and marina, some boat docks, a number of homes, a gigantic resort hotel with a smaller one adjacent, and a magnificent golf course. One can drive around all the streets of Windermere in less than five minutes.

Yet Windermere is more than it seems. By boat it is unmistakable, dominated by the vast and lovely Windermere House, one of the oldest landmarks on Lake Rosseau. It is also a summer home to several hundred cottagers, and a kind of spiritual oasis to thousands more. Ojibwas have camped and traded there. Countless couples have been married there. Thousands have honeymooned there. No doubt thousands have spent the best days of their lives there. It is a place where musicians have performed, artists have drawn inspiration, poets and philosophers have ruminated, and young lovers have strolled amid its trees and lawns and gardens on quiet moonlit evenings for five or six generations. This is no ordinary village!

A HAYRIDE FOR GUESTS AT FIFE HOUSE.
(NAC PA159524)

There is something captivating about Windermere. Perhaps it is partly the beautiful, parklike setting on the tiny bay, overlooking the lovely panorama of Lake Rosseau. Perhaps it is the timeless, old-fashioned magnificence of Windermere House, one of the last of Muskoka's splendid "grand hotels." But surely much of its charm comes from the atmosphere of the place. Windermere is a genuinely relaxed, unspoiled little community where the pace of life is placid, people are pleasant and friendly, everyone knows everyone else, and visitors are made to feel welcome. No wonder it exerts such a magnetic appeal.

Windermere is one of Ontario's best-loved resort villages. It also has the distinction of being the oldest European community on Lake Rosseau, and briefly the most prominent. It was the first local sawmill centre. It was once an important transshipping point, back in the days of stages and steamboats. It once had five or six resorts. Windermere has a story worthy of being told. Here it is.

An early charcoal sketch of Windermere House, ca. 1888.

• CHAPTER 1 •

THE EARLY DAYS (1860–1896)

ALMOST ALL EVENTS AT WINDERMERE prior to the 1860s are lost in the mists of time. However, from historical and geological records, it is possible to reconstruct a few facts.

For example, we know that, until about ten thousand years ago, the site of Windermere — and indeed all of Ontario — was buried beneath the immense glaciers of the Wisconsin ice sheet. After the glaciers retreated, a huge meltwater lake, now known as Lake Algonquin, filled much of modern Michigan and Ontario, until the land, rid of the crushing weight of the ice, rebounded and caused Lake Algonquin to drain by way of the Mississippi and Trent Rivers. The giant lake made its mark, however, by depositing thick alluvial layers over the Precambrian bedrock, thus resulting in the clay belts of Monck, Ryde and Watt Townships, which today comprise the finest farming lands in Muskoka.

As the climate warmed up and the subarctic tundra gave way to birches and poplars, and later pine, spruce, oak, and maple forests, small bands of aboriginal hunter-gatherers found their way into Muskoka. Perhaps some of them camped occasionally at Windermere Bay, but time has eradicated any trace of their presence. Undoubtedly the Ojibwas must have made frequent use of the easy overland route from Portage Bay to Three Mile Lake, from which there is ready access to Mary Lake and the Lake of Bays, but there is no reason to believe that they ever settled permanently in Muskoka until the nineteenth century. By the 1830s there was a Native settlement on Tobin Island, and at Port Carling a little later. Certainly a number of people — including Chief Mesqua-Ukee, who gave his name to the Muskoka District, and the shadowy fur-trader Jean-Baptiste Rousseau, for whom Lake Rosseau is named, and William Robinson of Penetanguishene, who operated from his cabin at Yoho Island on Lake Joseph, and the immortal mapmaker David Thompson — all visited the site of Windermere, but the whole region remained what it had always been: a vast Native hunting ground.

SKINNER FAMILY HAYING NEAR CLARK'S FALLS, WINDERMERE, ONTARIO. MR. SKINNER SR., TOM CLARK, MR. HARDY, MRS. CLARK, FLORENCE SKINNER, WALTER AND MILDRED, BABY DOROTHY SKINNER, MABEL SKINNER, MRS. SKINNER, WILLIE SKINNER, MRS. JEANNE PETTIT.

All this began to change around the middle of the nineteenth century, when the Canadian government became profoundly aware of the need for additional farming lands to lure in more immigrants. Consequently, ignoring the warnings of critics, it ordered surveys of the Ottawa-Huron Tract, that vast expanse of hills and lakes and forests lying north of the Severn River and the Kawartha Lakes, and started advertising in Britain, Germany, and other countries that free lands were available to would-be settlers. It also ordered a number of "colonization roads" to be slashed through the wilderness, providing access to the new Eden.

That the colonization scheme was basically a mistake — that the critics were right in claiming that most of the region consisted of sterile granite, and that hundreds of men and women tragically wasted their time, money, energies and even their lives trying to tame a region where it was impossible to farm profitably — is now history. On the positive side, the effort did lay the basis of the modern Muskoka, and also gave rise to the Village of Windermere.

By the year 1862 the Muskoka Road, the most successful of the colonization roads, had been extended north from Washago, past the future sites of Gravenhurst and Bracebridge to Falkenburg, where one of the district's first post offices was opened in 1863. In 1864 the Parry Sound Road, branching off at Falkenburg, was opened to Parry Sound, past the north side of Three Mile Lake. Two years later it was declared fit for wheeled vehicles. Soon a van or wagon, known locally as the "Black Maria," was bumping its way painfully over the road twice a week, carrying mail and passengers, but for most of its length it was little better than a stumpy trail. In any case, many land-hungry settlers did not wait for the roads, or even the surveyors. As early as 1862, years before Watt Township was laid out, a genial pioneer named Jacob "Jake" Bogart, of Pennsylvania Dutch Loyalist ancestry, was building a shanty beside a creek flowing into the southeast side of Three Mile Lake, thus becoming the founder of the small farming community of Ufford.

More newcomers followed. In 1863 came James M. Shea and his family, second-generation Irish immigrants from Glengarry County. The Sheas settled west of Jake Bogart's holdings and began clearing the land and erecting their own shanty. It was an exceedingly rugged life they led, amid bitterly cold winters and the mosquitoes and blackflies of summer, without roads or transport facilities, or sawmills or gristmills, or even any stores or doctors or clergymen closer than Orillia. Wild animals were another problem: wolves might kill the occasional calf, or bears might take a sheep. Fortunately the Sheas knew how to fell trees, and chop wood, and hunt and trap and fish and tan deerskins and make soap from lye and improvise tools. They were hardy enough to walk fifty or more miles to get fresh provisions or mail a letter. They also knew how to deal with ruffians trying to drive them off their lands. Within a year they were joined by a few additional families, including the Hammels, who located near the northeast side of Three Mile Lake, and the Creasor brothers. By that time a sawmill and a gristmill had been built at North Falls (Bracebridge).

It did not take long for some of the new settlers to discover Lake Rosseau.

One of them was David Fife, a Scottish farmer from Peterborough County. Fife's father, also named David Fife, had already immortalized himself and revolutionized Canadian agriculture when, in 1842, he discovered a new strain of wheat, still known as Red Fife wheat, which is resistant to both frost and wheat rust. However, the Fife family was large, and land was running out in Otonabee Township. Consequently in 1863 the younger Fife, then aged thirty-four, decided to try Muskoka. Along with a few companions he trudged in all the way from Bobcaygeon over winter snows with a sleigh drawn by an ox team. After a difficult trek he selected what became Lot 29, Concession VIII, Watt, now in the heart of Windermere, and began building a log shanty. Fife then returned to Otonabee, and when the weather warmed he brought out his wife, the former Ellen Aitken, and their four young children. By 1868 they were able to have some of their logs sawn into lumber, and could then build a permanent home, some 36 by 20 feet in size, with a gabled roof — rather better than most early settlers could manage. Like most pioneers the Fifes did some logging and gradually developed a farm; later they purchased Lot 30 to the west as well, and paid for it by selling cordwood to be used as fuel by the local steamboats.

The example of David Fife was soon copied by his Otonabee neighbour Thomas Aitken. Little is known of Aitken's early life, except that he was born at Burra in the Shetland Islands in 1832 and worked as a boatbuilder and fisherman before emigrating to Canada with his siblings in 1860. For a time he settled in Peterborough County, perhaps because some of his cousins were there; some of them intermarried with the Fifes. Aitken was friendly with the Fifes, and in 1863 he likewise decided to go to Muskoka. He walked up the Muskoka Road, all the way from Washago to Watt, where he met Jake Bogart and confided that he wanted some land "as flat as a pancake." Bogart replied that he knew just the place and guided him westwards to the gently rolling, arable lands that now constitute the Windermere Golf Course. Thomas Aitken then selected what became Lot 25, Concession VIII and built a modest cabin on an elevated knoll (now called Beech Ridge Hill) just outside the modern village, but within a year David Fife induced him to move closer to the lake. Aitken finally settled on Lot 31, and erected his farmhouse on a hilltop sloping gently

THOMAS AITKEN FARMHOUSE, WINDERMERE.

down to Windermere Bay and commanding a lovely view of Lake Rosseau. It proved a most auspicious choice. Mr. Aitken did most of his clearing in the winters and meanwhile earned money on the side by working as a sailor on the Great Lakes — until he apparently ran afoul of some of the Fenians, who were then contemplating an attack on Canada, and had to flee for his life. Not until 1868 did he become a year-round resident of Windermere. His unmarried sister Elizabeth joined him, helping to keep house, and soon his farm was pasturing horses, cattle, sheep, and chickens. In 1872 he married a widow from Peterborough County, Mary Stanger Traill, whom he had known for many years; they had two children, William and Minnie.

The third founding resident of Windermere was Francis Forge, a hearty, breezy Yorkshireman born in 1838. A vigorous farmhand who never lost his old-country accent, Francis Forge left England at the age of eighteen and landed at New York City, where he was promptly robbed, but somehow he managed to find his way to York County, Canada West (now Ontario). Here he supported himself at various jobs around Unionville and Markham, and in 1862 married Elizabeth Jemima Dawson, although initially he had little to offer her except a share in his poverty. But in 1863 he heard that land was available in Muskoka, and carrying all of his meagre possessions in a cotton sack, he trekked up the Muskoka Road to Beatrice, about five miles north of Falkenburg, which was then at the outer fringe of settlement. Still dissatisfied, Forge soon headed west to Lake Rosseau, and liked what he saw. Here he met a squatter named Sanderson (or as some say, George Kirbyson) who had decided that Lake Rosseau was too remote. The two struck a deal and agreed to swap lands. Thus Francis Forge laid claim to Lot 28, Concession VIII, a lovely piece of land, sloping gently to the modern Forge's Bay, directly behind Wellesley Island, just east of the modern Village of Windermere. He soon brought out his wife and baby son, plus his brother-in-law William Dawson, who settled on the next lot, and his wife's crippled sister, Rachel.

Sustained by their staunch Methodist faith and Mr. Forge's unwavering optimism, the family, aided occasionally by their neighbours, gradually began clearing their lands, building barns, planting crops, and raising a few cattle, pigs, and sheep. In time eleven children were born, seven of whom survived. When Mr. Forge formally applied for his land patent in 1868, he was told that because his lot comprised less than two hundred acres, he could also have Island G (Wellesley) provided that he would pay an extra eleven dollars a year in taxes. Forge judged the island useless for growing potatoes, and rejected the offer — a decision he may have regretted in later years.

By that time the local settlers received another great boon, in the form of a sawmill, which was built by an Englishman named Archibald Taylor at the mouth of the Dee River, about a mile north of Windermere. The site, though rather remote by land, offers excellent waterpower, and soon logs were being fed down the Dee River from Three Mile Lake, or boomed and poled along the shores of Lake Rosseau when the winds were favourable, to be turned into planks that were sleighed, teamed, or rafted out. In January 1868 a post office was opened, and given the name of "Windermere," perhaps at Taylor's suggestion. (The name "Windermere" is derived from the famous lake and resort village in northern England, famed as the home of the poet William Wordsworth.) The post office was assigned to John McAlpine of Utterson, who contented himself with delivering the mailbag to Taylor's home, but Taylor soon tired of the responsibility of distributing the mail and asked Thomas Aitken to look after it. McAlpine resigned his position in March 1869, and Aitken officially succeeded him a year later. The mill and the post office turned Windermere into a place of pilgrimage by the local settlers.

Despite the efforts of the Watt settlers, the Muskoka colonization scheme was not doing very well, and by 1865 there was even talk of abandoning the entire effort. Help, however, was on the way. In 1866 Mr. A. P. Cockburn, a Victoria County merchant, founded a stage service from Washago to Gravenhurst, and also built a steamboat, the *Wenonah*, which he used to ferry passengers and freight and the Royal Mail to Bracebridge and other points on Lake Muskoka. Thrice weekly the *Wenonah* — barring an accident — also travelled to the Native village at Baisong Rapids (Port Carling). Soon there was a small store at Port Carling, and also a local mail service to Ashdown village, near the head of Lake Rosseau, utilizing a skiff or sailboat. Lake Rosseau was becoming less isolated! In 1867 Cockburn was elected to the Ontario legislature as the first MPP for Muskoka, and soon persuaded the government to revise its immigration policies, and to survey additional lands for settlement. The result, in 1868, was the Free Grant and Homesteads Act, which resulted in a considerable influx of new settlers. At the same time it was announced that eleven new townships, including Watt, were to be opened under the terms of the Act.

The surveys assigned Watt Township an area of 47,283 acres, of which 12,057 were water, and within a decade most of its lands had been claimed, if not settled. In 1869 the small steamer *Waubamik* made her first appearance on Lake Rosseau, and by 1871 a lock had been completed past the Baisong Rapids, allowing the boats to make through trips from Gravenhurst. The first election rally at Windermere took place in 1872, when Mr. Cockburn, now running to represent Muskoka in Ottawa, arrived aboard the *Nipissing* on his way to Rosseau. At both places he addressed a large crowd, and the loud ovations he received seemed to assure victory.

With the coming of the steamers, activity increased at Portage Bay, which seemed likely to become the main unloading site on eastern Lake Rosseau. This did not satisfy Thomas Aitken, who wanted the boats to call at Windermere instead. To bring this about, he arranged to build a wharf at his own expense, but the steamboat crews were not overly impressed with it. Windermere Bay offers poor shelter, from either the northwest or southwest winds, and it is said that only the promise of cordwood on a regular basis induced A. P. Cockburn to use the new dock. This meant that the summer mail was being delivered directly to Mr. Aitken's home, which was now the post office.

The next factor in the equation was, of course, a road to link the new landing with the interior of Watt, and Thomas Aitken did his best to provide one. Meanwhile, in 1871 Watt and Cardwell became a jointly incorporated township, and one of the first moves by the new council was to order a road blazed around the south side of Three Mile Lake, through Ufford (which itself received a post office in 1870), and connecting with the Parry Sound Road about ten miles north of Bracebridge. The road — which is now the Windermere Road — was laid out by William Shea and his neighbour William Kay, and on Kay's advice the route ran right over the top of a hill about four miles east of Windermere (rather than around it). On first seeing it, Frank Forge made a comment that the hill was so steep that a man would need to thank God for having reached the top — with the result that it is known as "Thanksgiving Hill" to this day, although in recent years the top has been shaved off by the Department of Highways. By the early 1870s, as long as the lakes remained open, Ufford, Raymond and Ullswater regularly received their mail from Windermere three days a week.

A stage service was required to move mail, freight, and passengers. A double-seated democrat was used in the warmer seasons, and a double sleigh in winter. It was an unenviable job. Frequently the teamsters would have to rise about four o'clock on a bitterly cold winter morning to have some hot porridge, feed and water their teams, and harness them up so as to be on the roads by five o'clock. After 1886 the stages ran from Windermere to as far as Falkenburg, on a round trip of about thirty-five miles over some considerable hills, although a winter road was commonly improvised across some of the swamps. Often there would be a few passengers along for the ride: that was part of the contract, and indeed the only other way out of Windermere in the wintertime was to walk four miles across the ice to Port Carling, taking care to avoid the dangerous ice on the Indian River. At Falkenburg there might be a wait of four or five hours for the northbound train from Toronto. A few grocery staples, such as flour and sugar, might be collected, and the teamsters would head home again. Sometimes the sleigh might also be used to take the local children to school when the weather was unusually cold.

It is not certain who originally ran the Windermere stages, but in 1896 David Fife Junior was awarded the contract, and would always set off all wrapped up in his coonskin coat, fur-lined cap, and woollen mittens. The sleigh was warmed with hot slabs of wood wrapped in burlap, or perhaps a few hot-water footwarmers made of tin; otherwise, people had to make do with heavy Saskatchewan robes. The horses, Maude and Tip, were decked out with sets of body bells, and their tails were plaited and tied high to avoid freezing. They served for a total of eighteen years, and only once failed to complete a trip — on a particularly stormy day, when the snowdrifts defied all efforts to push or scrap through them. In 1899 James Fife, one of David's sons, took over the job, and three years later his brother Stuart took charge. Around 1914 William Aitken assumed the contract. The stages were still running as late as 1928, and also connecting at Utterson, but by then they were giving way to trucks, while crews were starting to plow the winter roads. No wonder the villagers always eagerly awaited the breakup of the ice every spring, when the shrill whistle of the returning steamboat announced that winter's reign was finally over.

Despite the efforts of the Aitkens, little happened at Windermere landing for many more years, except that the settlers' clearings grew steadily larger, stumps disappeared, and one or two warehouses were built. Perhaps the inhabitants preferred it thus: the Windermere settlers had come out to farm, not to form a village. If anything, the anticipated "town" seemed likely to appear elsewhere, on the banks of the Dee.

The upper Dee River, which drains Three Mile Lake, in many ways seemed an admirable site for a town. It lies amid some of the finest farms in Watt; it was already served by a road (which originally crossed the river over two bridges at the top of the falls); and it possesses fine waterpower, in the form of two cascades spilling over the rocks below the lake. It is also located just one and a quarter miles from Portage Bay, or two miles from Windermere. Given all these advantages, it was almost inevitable that this fine millsite would be put to use, and in 1868 — if we may believe local tradition — an Englishman named John Shannon (or Shennan) arrived, sized up the prospects, and arranged to build a sawmill on the north bank, just at the foot of the upper chutes. The mill was speedily followed by a timber slide to get the logs safely past the falls, plus a dam downstream to create a millpond. A fine two-storey home was built for the Shannon family.

The next step was an urgently needed gristmill, and Shannon engaged an old-country English contractor named Frank Newel to build it. Newel soon had almost all the timbers cut, according to a plan which existed only in his own mind, but then Shannon very unwisely began to ask a lot of questions and get in the way. Newel was not a man to brook any interference. The two men came to blows, and the angry builder packed up his tools and left for Saginaw, Michigan. No one had the remotest idea how to assemble the timbers, and soon Mr. Shannon was desperately trying to locate Newel and lure him back. It took most of a year, and even required a personal trip to Saginaw, but finally the cantankerous carpenter agreed to come back and finish the job. Finding hands to help was no problem: most of the men of Watt, including the Sheas, Bogarts, Pickerings, Kingshotts, Bill Russell, Bill "British" Bateman, William Kay, Robert Giles, James Gott and John Oldham, took part in the raising, along with Alex "Sandy" Fraser of Brackenrig and Thomas Aitken, David Fife and Archie Taylor of Windermere. No pay was offered, but there was plenty of food; even so, the mills cost at least two thousand dollars. When completed, the building stood at least three and a half storeys tall, on stone foundations, and was reckoned one of the finest north of Orillia. (It was also the only one north of Bracebridge.) The machinery was supplied by the well-known firm of Goldie and McCulloch. Once the job was done, everyone celebrated by holding a dance and singalong, with Mr. Bateman soloing on several Irish ballads. Mr. Shannon was meanwhile fortunate to secure the services of Louis Klingbeil as handyman at the mills in 1871. Klingbeil was a master machinist who had emigrated from Berlin, Germany, to Montreal in 1869 with his family, before answering an advertisement to work at Dee Bank; later he bought a farm from Shannon north of the river and east of the mills, and there established a blacksmith shop.

Despite the occasional problem with low waters, insufficient trained hands, or illnesses in the Shannon family, the Dee Bank mills were soon very busy, even attracting customers from as far away as Parry Sound. Mr. Shannon soon built several houses for his millhands; one old-timer recalls seeing the ruins of about twelve or fifteen of them along the river's north shore. Meanwhile a store and hotel appeared along the west side of the road, north of the river, on land owned by Thomas Huggard, who had moved in from Manitoulin Island. Around 1873 a small log school, about 20 by 30 feet in size, was built on the hilltop west of the Dee Bank Road, south of the river; the rear end of the building had to be supported by several five-foot posts to keep it level. Ernie Bogart, a cousin of Jake, was apparently the first teacher. A post office followed in 1874 (probably in the store) and was assigned to A. B. Shannon; later it went to a John Friser and thence to John M. Barber in 1880. About that time James M. Barber (perhaps the same man) erected a tannery a little further downstream. We also hear of a second store and a shingle mill. Around 1878 a frame Presbyterian church was built, at the corner of Dee Bank Road and Windermere Road; in 1897 this structure was bricked and converted into a new school as the original became dilapidated. Thus Dee Bank Village became a thriving little industrial centre; together with Windermere, it was reckoned to have a population of sixty souls in 1878, as compared to one hundred in Ullswater and fifty in Ufford.

Faced with all this competition at its back door, Windermere landing remained almost stagnant throughout the 1870s. Matters were not helped by the fact that the entire country was in the grip of a severe economic depression from 1873 until 1878, which badly hurt the lumber trade and discouraged the infant tourist industry. In 1880 Archibald Taylor sold his sawmill and took up a new career as a grocer in York County. The property, including most of four lots along the (unbuilt) ninth concession, soon passed to George Hutcheson, who was already an experienced sawmiller. Since Hutcheson sold the property in 1885 for four thousand dollars, at four times the purchase price, we may conclude that he rebuilt the mill.

What really brought Windermere to life was the tourist industry. This was inspired largely by A. P. Cockburn, who was one of the first to realize that the rocks, hills, lakes, and islands of Muskoka might make ideal recreation terrain for sportsmen, campers, and fishermen who were getting tired of the noise, smog, and grime of the new industrial cities, and longing for a temporary "return to Nature." All that was needed, he felt, was advertising to promote the district's charms and suitable accommodations. Accessibility was no longer a problem: after 1875 visitors could travel from Toronto to Gravenhurst directly

WINDERMERE HOUSE AND WHARF, CA. 1890. (EDWIN PAULLETTE)

by rail, and then take a steamer from Muskoka Wharf all through the lakes. Consequently Mr. Cockburn devoted much time every winter to writing pamphlets and press releases and touring parts of the United States, extolling the attractions of Muskoka as a tourist paradise. He also encouraged settlers located close to the lakes to open their homes to summer visitors. For a long time the results were meagre, and until about 1880 the only real tourist hotels were William Pratt's Rosseau House at Rosseau village, and the Summit House at Port Cockburn on Lake Joseph.

Then the idea began to catch on. More and more campers and sportsmen (mostly Americans) began arriving at the steamboat landings, and then pestering the local settlers with questions as to the best fishing grounds, or where one could get a good shoot. They might also ask permission to borrow a rowboat or pitch their tents on the settlers' lands. Soon they were also asking for bacon, eggs, milk, bread, and other foodstuffs, and perhaps a roof over their heads for the night. Every year they kept coming back, in larger and larger numbers, and they offered cash for what they consumed. The farmers were delighted to have new customers, especially since money is usually scarce in a pioneer economy, and though the settlers might have secretly resented these rich presumptuous city slickers, both soon realized how useful the other might be to them. Gradually some of the settlers began building additions to their homes, and as the visitors kept coming they continued to build. In time settlers' homes turned into summer boarding houses, and some of these in turn evolved into resort hotels. As early as 1879 Richard Penson of Port Carling was turning his home at Ferndale into a small hotel. In 1882 the Cox family of Port Sandfield opened the Prospect House, and by 1883 C. J. Minett was starting to turn his farm across the lake into Clevelands House, now the largest resort on Lake Rosseau. Opportunity was beckoning.

ELIZABETH BOYER AND THOMAS AITKEN. (FLORENCE AITKEN)

It is said that Thomas Aitken of Windermere built a few cabins for tourists as early as 1872, but this seems unlikely. His wife had recently died, and furthermore, Mr. Aitken was a rather rigid, aloof, retiring farmer, not especially keen on socializing. Almost certainly he occasionally provided quarters for transients (as most settlers did), but he does not seem to have responded to the tourist trend in a serious way until 1883. By that time he apparently had at least two houses, of which his own was a substantial 20 by 30 feet. It is certain that he formally bought four and a half acres of extra land from the Fifes in March 1883 and began advertising that his home at Windermere could accommodate about thirty summer guests. He had built a new three-storey boarding-house wing, about 43 by 32 feet, complete with a new kitchen, onto the back of his two-storey home, plus bathhouses near the beach. His son William, aided by a neighbour, used a team of oxen borrowed from Alfred Judd of Juddhaven to help pile the stones for the foundations; the yoke was later kept as a souvenir. The family soon moved into the new wing, which also housed the post office. At first the premises was simply called the Aitken House, but as the guests kept coming, the boarding house soon swelled into a summer hotel, and a new name was required. A travelogue written in 1886 notes that

"Windermere is pleasantly situated on a small bay, four miles [by boat] from Port Carling and ten miles from Rosseau," and that the Windermere House (as it now was) had "large accommodation and increasing business," so much so that around 1888, Mr. Aitken added another new three-storey section to the front. This portion measured 65 by 33 feet. Like most Muskoka hotelkeepers, he also acted as postmaster and express agent, as well as local adviser on baits and fishing. Most of the food and produce used by the hotel came from the Aitken farm, which was gradually taken over by William, who ran it until 1912. The guests, of course, always arrived by steamer, usually the *Muskoka* or the *Kenozha* during the 1880s. Right from the very start Windermere House was described as "quiet and respectable": in 1887 a correspondent for the *Toronto World* noted the "good taste in furnishings and exquisite neatness [that] are characteristic of the place," and went on to praise the roomy halls, parlours, and airy chambers. He concluded by saying that there was "nothing lacking

FIFE HOUSE (RIGHT), NEWLY BUILT, CA. 1888. WINDERMERE HOUSE (LEFT). NOTE THAT THE BACK WING OF WINDERMERE HOUSE WAS BUILT FIRST, AS AN ADDITION TO THE AITKEN HOME.

which can give an added zest to enjoyment." The rates were then six to seven dollars per week, with half rates for children under ten. The tone of the new hotel was probably set largely by Thomas Aitken's second wife, Elizabeth Boyer of Bracebridge, who did much of the actual work of running it. No cards or liquor were allowed.

By 1879 a few individuals were already eyeing Windermere as a place to build a summer home or cottage. One of the first was George Paton of Toronto, whose family was associated with the Dominion Bank. The Patons had gotten into the habit of boarding with the Fife family during the summers, and in 1879 Mr. Paton purchased the promontory northwest of Windermere House from Thomas Aitken. Four years later Paton and six associates organized a company called the Windermere Club, with himself as president, to rent or sell cabins. Part of the idea was to have a central clubhouse with dining facilities, but this was never implemented. That same year the club sold a fourteen-acre headland about a mile north of Windermere to Alexander Nairn, one of the partners, who built a cottage and named the site Nairn's Point. (Much later it would become the famous Llanllar estate, one of the loveliest properties on Lake Rosseau.) Paton also established a Mechanics Institute in Windermere, organized by his wife, and patterned after the parent organization in Great Britain, which was dedicated to improving the lot of working people. The building apparently stood adjacent to the modern Anglican church, and by 1886 it already had a reading room and a small library; perhaps some of the summer visitors provided the books and periodicals. It seems to have lasted until the 1890s, but evidently petered out and perhaps died for lack of staffing. In 1886 Paton Point (then known as Harcourt Point, after one of Paton's partners) was subdivided into eighteen lots and a network of paper "streets," of which only one, Cameron Avenue, actually exists today, as a mere lane. Some shoreline lots were sold to such families as the Andersons, who were related to the Patons, and later their in-laws, the Duncans, but the interior plots remained vacant; the club failed to make a metropolis of Windermere. Cottages soon arose, many of which were built by the resident master carpenter, Julius Klingbeil — perhaps a cousin of Louis. The Patons themselves built two chalets, while the Andersons built the Bungalow in 1888. Patterned after those in India, the cottage has wide verandahs and lofty ceilings, and today it is one of the oldest surviving summer homes on Lake Rosseau.

In the meantime Windermere was growing. Around 1880 Henry Ditchburn, who had previously opened a boat livery at Rosseau, put up a boathouse east of Windermere wharf, and used it to rent or sell punts, skiffs, and rowboats which he built himself. They were soon much in demand by the tourists, who used them for fishing or picnics at various islands, or to go over to Portage Bay, where there was a fine beach. (Canoes were very rare until the 1890s.) In 1885 John Robert Boyd, who may have operated the old Taylor sawmill for a time, acquired a lot on Windermere Road from David Fife and speedily erected the community's first store, located close to the modern Windermere House garage. Around the same time he also took over Ditchburn's boat livery.

RELIGIOUS LIFE IN THE NEW SETTLEMENT was also receiving attention. As early as 1865 an itinerant Primitive Methodist missionary, the Reverend Patteson, who was responsible for bringing the word of God to the entire territory between Severn Bridge and Huntsville, was making the occasional call at Ufford. The Windermere settlers all attended services there, but crop failures in 1871 and 1872 left them without enough money to sustain their church. However, the Fifes soon offered their home as a temporary place of worship, and now and then the occasional travelling minister was known to call, on any day of the week, sometimes after dark. The family would put him up for the night, and the following morning David Fife Junior would bring the news to the neighbours. The only musical instrument at these impromptu services was a tuning fork, but the Fifes and the Forges knew how to carry a tune!

In 1884 Windermere became a mission, and plans were made to build a church. It was started in the heart of the modern village, on land donated by David Fife, but progress was very slow; before the winter they had a building up but could not complete it. A renewed effort was made the following summer. Thanks to gifts of lumber, more gratis work by the settlers, and fundraising teas and concerts held by the ladies (plus donations from the summer people), the building's interior gradually took shape. By the winter of 1887 it was complete, with stove and lights. An organ was soon procured, with Mrs. John Boyd doing the first honours.

The new church served both settlers and tourists alike but by 1892 it was found to be too small. Another plot of land adjacent to the

WINDERMERE HOUSE, DITCHBURN LIVERY, AND FIFE HOUSE AT WINDERMERE, ONTARIO. (FLORENCE AITKEN)

first was obtained from David Fife, and in 1893 work was started on a new church. By 1894 it was ready, and as usual it was a community effort. The new church measured about 60 by 40 feet and had plastered interior walls with a four-foot wainscoting, and an entry porch. It also featured a stone foundation. Around 1899 a brick parsonage was also provided across the road for the minister. This building is still one of the landmarks of Windermere.

Sunday school was another regular feature of community life. It was conducted in the original church building (which also served as a community hall), and every summer a picnic for the children was held on the grounds outside. Within a few years, however, it became the custom for all the local church schools — and many of the people — to take an excursion on one of the Navigation Company steamers, usually to Port Cockburn or Bala Park Island, where sports and a picnic would be held. An organ would be loaded aboard at Windermere, and each local Sunday school choir competed for a prize. (As a rule, the Ufford school won, thanks to the singing talents of Adam Veitch and his family.) In later years, when steamship cruises went out of style, local picnics were resumed, often on the Fife House grounds. Every winter there was a Christmas party; Santa always attended, and brought a gift for every child. In 1897 the Presbyterian church at Dee Bank was closed and re-established at Windermere, across the road from the modern Anglican church. It was a white, frame building with a bell tower, and remained open until 1925, when most Presbyterian and Methodist congregations in Canada merged to form the United Church of Canada.

In the midst of all these developments, the Fifes likewise decided to go into the resort business. Since 1882 David Fife Junior had been engaged in clearing land at his new farm on Portage Bay, though he did not live there. That same December he married Mary Ann Galloway,

S.S. *Ethel May*, CA. 1890. FRANK FORGE (OWNER, LEFT), WILLIAM FORGE (CAPTAIN), MRS. FORGE (PASSENGER), AND MR. COPPING (ENGINEER). (DOROTHY DUKE)

whom he had met while working at her parents' farm east of Ullswater. The Fifes were used to hosting visitors, sometimes even sacrificing their own beds and sleeping in the barn to accommodate them. In the fall of 1887 David Fife Junior, age thirty, bought a piece of his father's property for the princely sum of one dollar, and immediately engaged Julius Klingbeil to supervise construction of another hotel. David Fife Senior, who was an excellent carpenter and framer, assisted with the job. Work continued all winter, and by the following spring the new building was ready.

The Fife House was a modest-sized, white-painted resort, with three storeys, a gabled roof with dormers, and (in later years) green shingles and a large verandah. Set amid a grove of trees, it faced directly onto the beach at Windermere Bay, on lower ground than its neighbour. After the first few seasons it was decorated with a little gingerbread trim, and a covered balcony was added to the second floor. Inside the main entrance was a hall leading to the main stairway, and further on, to Mr. Fife's office. To the right was a spacious dining room offering a fine view of the bay, while to the left was a large lounge used for concerts, dances, and card parties. The guest quarters were, of course, on the two upper floors, which contained twenty-seven bedrooms. Amenities were initially rather primitive: the mattresses were ticks stuffed with straw, water had to be hauled in barrels from the lake or a well on a sleigh or "jumper," and lighting took the form of siche safety gas, but in those days guests did not expect all the comforts of home. At the rear were the family quarters and the kitchen. Cooking was done on a pair of large, wood-fired cook stoves, though after ten years these were

GUESTS AT WINDERMERE HOUSE, CA. 1890.

replaced by a double range with double fireboxes and ovens. The Fife House then took about sixty guests. Mrs. Fife ran the kitchen, and we are assured that the meals and pastries prepared therein were mouthwatering.

David and Mary Ann Fife proved to be admirable hosts, and their new hotel seldom had a vacant room. Its success prompted Thomas Aitken to make even more improvements to Windermere House, and in 1889 he built a whole new front and tower onto his former residence, which was now completely swallowed up; what had formerly been the Aitken home now became the front office, foyer and lounge in the big hotel. Many members of the family worked there, including Mr. Aitken's daughter-in-law Annie Matilda Forge (who married William), and his step-daughter, Mary Traill. By 1887 Windermere House was already taking one hundred guests; one of them, Harry Hobbs, later to be president of the Ferry-Morris Feed Company of Detroit, kept coming for forty-five seasons!

CANOEISTS AT WINDERMERE, ON LAKE ROSSEAU.

Of course the rise of the resorts spelled all sorts of new opportunities for the local people. The hotels required housekeepers, laundresses, porters, cooks, waiters, and groundskeepers, to say nothing of carpenters, painters, and mechanics. Many a local boy learned a new trade and many a girl was able to land a job in the city, thanks to one of the guests. In addition to the family, around eight to ten local girls were employed at the Fife House alone; one girl might be responsible for making up four to five rooms daily. Some of the hotel staff worked long hours and were poorly paid, but with luck they could rely on tips. Thomas Aitken himself made relatively little money from his hotel; most of his profits were spent on maintaining and improving it.

Around 1885 Francis Forge also decided to cater to the tourists, albeit in a different way. Noting that it was sometimes difficult for campers and cottagers to get to town to buy groceries, he decided on a novel venture: a supply-boat service to bring foodstuffs directly to the campers and cottagers. Mr. Forge may have been the first man in Muskoka to try it. He started out with a large dugout (which was

THOMAS CLARK'S SAWMILL, CLARK'S FALLS, DEE RIVER. (JEANNE.PETTIT)

soon exchanged for a rowboat), and early in the mornings he would load up his boat with all sorts of fresh garden greens and fruits and freshly slaughtered lamb cuts, and then row all around Lake Rosseau, calling on the tourists, who were usually glad to see him. Since this took up a lot of his time, Forge soon began buying some of his victuals from the local farmers. In time he built up an extensive list of customers, and even extended his runs to Lake Joseph. Seldom would he get back home until late at night, usually heralding his return with a lusty song.

In 1888 he imported a little steamboat called the *Ethel May*, which was 30 feet in length and registered at 2.46 tons, and used her to peddle his provisions; his eldest son, William, usually took charge. The *Ethel May* was far more commodious than the rowboat, and had cabins to provide shelter from the rain, but she was also more expensive to run and required a qualified engineer. Besides that, William Hanna of Port Carling was fitting out the much larger steamer *Mink* for the same purpose in 1891. Perhaps for such reasons, Forge sold the *Ethel* in 1891 and resumed the use of the rowboat. Thus the *Ethel May* was

SCENE AT WINDERMERE, CA. 1895. THE STEAMER *Muskoka* IS AT THE WHARF. JOHNSTON'S BOAT LIVERY AND THE FIFE HOUSE ARE AT RIGHT.

probably the first engine-driven craft to ply from Windermere.

The tourist industry continued to grow. By 1890 there were about fifteen resort hotels all around the Muskoka Lakes, and still the number grew. 1893 was said to have been a record year, with every resort packed to the rafters; some guests paid money just to sleep in the hall corridors. Around 1890 a windmill was installed to pump water up to a holding tank on the roof of Windermere House (which was now fitted out with pipes) although the new device was useless on a calm day. In 1893 Mr. Aitken also added a new bowling green in front of the hotel, soon to be followed by tennis courts; more and more, the guests expected to be amused as well as accommodated. The following year he sent his son William to Owen Sound to learn telegraphy — which probably means that a telegraph office was opened at the hotel about that time. The guests commonly amused themselves with strolling, fishing, and bathing (swimming per se was not considered quite respectable at that time!), and with campfires, dancing, and singalongs in the evenings. Every so often an excursion might be arranged on one of the Navigation Company steamers, such as the *Kenozha* or the *Medora*; this would allow for visits to other hotels or attendance at regattas, which became more and more popular as the number of boats grew. Many were held at Windermere, starting in the 1880s, and attracted tourists and local people alike.

Thus, within a mere decade, Windermere landing blossomed into a real village. Around 1891 Catherine Eleanor Inglis of Toronto purchased John R. Boyd's store, and seems to have run it for several years, with some help from her husband, John, who worked at the Clark sawmill. Perhaps the opening of a rival store in 1896 led to financial difficulties: in 1897 her creditors took over the property and sold it to her husband. Perhaps at this time Mrs. Inglis engaged her husband to convert the store into a small hotel, known as the Ingleside House. Little is known of this resort today. It stood at the site of the modern Windermere House garage and old-timers vaguely recall it as a two-storey clapboard building, variously painted white or green, with a peaked roof and dormers and a front verandah. It had no access to the lake, and probably offerred only rooms and meals. By 1903 it was taking forty guests.

Meanwhile cottages were proliferating too. In 1886 the actor Billy Florence purchased Island F on Lake Rosseau, just south of Wellesley, and renamed it Florence Island. Mr. Florence did not stay long, however, and in 1890 his island was subdivided into nineteen lots. On the mainland the Reverend William Henry Hincks bought a cottage lot from David Fife Senior in 1897, opposite the Fife House, and named it Brownies' Bluff; today it is known as Tintagel. His son, Dr. Clare Hincks, spent many a summer at Windermere, where he was very popular, and later bought the Cringan cottage on Maple Leaf Bay; later still he would found the Mental Health Association of Canada. As early as 1881 Francis Forge sold a shoreline lot to George H. Suckling for twenty-five dollars and a larger one five years later to Reuben Millichamp for one hundred dollars. In 1887 Mr. Forge subdivided the point immediately south of Windermere House into building lots, and gradually sold off thirteen of them over the next twenty-five years, to such people as William Ingram, the Reverend Charles Henry Mockridge, and — most prominently — Timothy Eaton, the rising Toronto department store magnate who had long been spending his summers at Windermere House. Eaton acquired four and a half acres in 1896 and speedily built a large summer estate called Ravenscrag, facing Windermere Bay. It was staffed by about six or eight servants, including a lady in waiting for Mrs. Eaton. The servants boarded at Ravenscrag, while the non-domestic help — including the painters and carpenters — stayed at the Fife House. Francis Forge was engaged as caretaker (mainly a winter job) and used some of the proceeds to build himself a new house on his farm in 1895. As befitted their status, the Eatons also imported a number of steam yachts: the *Wapenao* (3.07 tons) in 1895, and the *Wanda* (7.87 tons) from Toronto in 1898. The latter vessel was 53.5 feet in length, had a torpedo stern, and was built for speed. Sometimes the Eatons would engage her to meet the trains at Muskoka Wharf, or to call at the homes of neighbouring cottagers. Sometimes Mrs. Margaret Eaton would host elegant little parties on board, with maids to serve tea, and cucumber sandwiches. The yachts, of course, required several men to operate them and a huge boathouse. Bertram Campbell was the captain and Matthew D. McCrone the engineer (aided by one or two firemen), and they always kept the yachts immaculate. Both men took up residence at nearby Forge's Bay, and both worked for the Eatons in Toronto over the winters. In 1904 Mr. Eaton sold the *Wanda* after she failed to win a race, and purchased the *Wanda II* (32.62 tons) which lasted until she was destroyed in a spectacular boathouse fire on August 6, 1914. (The *Wapeneo* was saved from the blaze, though slightly scorched, and was later converted into a motorboat.) Mrs. Eaton, by this time a widow, replaced her with the *Wanda III* (37.59 tons), a very similar vessel which she kept until 1930. The *Wanda III* still cruises on the Muskoka Lakes from Gravenhurst.

Cottage development was also proceeding further north. In 1899 the Reverend Elmore Harris of Toronto purchased Nairn's Point for fourteen hundred dollars (four times the original price). He also imported a big Polson steam yacht called the *Llano* (9.38 tons) which he used for nine years, before selling both the estate and the yacht to Joseph I. Irwin, a prominent industrialist from Columbus, Indiana, for the enormous sum of fifteen thousand dollars! The Irwins, who had previously spent their holidays camping on an island in Lake Joseph, turned the property into the lovely Llanllar (sunset) estate, with a huge multi-roomed cottage set on a lofty hilltop. Once it even had a windmill to pump in the water. Servants were imported every summer, along with a cow to provide fresh milk. The grounds, which cover thirty acres, were laid out like a natural park, and the shoreline festooned with flower gardens, which could be seen and admired from all the passing boats. Sometimes the Irwins would invite the general public in for picnics. Mr. Irwin himself was a quiet, retiring man who never put on airs, although he controlled several major corporations and for a time was governor of Indiana. He kept Llanllar right up to his death in 1939.

It seems ironic that the spectacular rise in the resort industry, which depended on the natural scenic attractions of Muskoka, also coincided with the heyday of the Muskoka lumber trade: sawmillers were still waging a relentless war of extermination against the pine. Every year boom timbers enclosing up to a thousand logs each were floated across Three Mile Lake to the mill at Dee Bank, or to Nathaniel Bogart's mill at Ufford, or to Lake Rosseau, along with similar drives from Skeleton Lake and all the local rivers, and even these accumulations were nothing compared with the mile-wide booms being towed across Lake Rosseau to Port Carling. Cedar was also cut for shingles, while countless farmers made money on the side by splitting and peeling cords of hemlock bark, which they hauled using horses and wagons (or sleighs in winter) to Portage Bay. There they would be loaded onto huge scows and taken to the tanneries at Bracebridge in the tow of tugs such as the *Rosseau*, the *Southwood*, and the *Queen of the Isles*. Somehow the setting of Windermere remained relatively cut off from these activities, although the village still had its own sawmill.

The Windermere sawmill, apparently rebuilt after 1880 by George Hutcheson, was doing a flourishing business. In 1885 it was sold to Thomas Clark and his brother Abraham, who were already experienced millers. Born in Nottingham, England, Clark had been brought to Canada as an infant. He grew up near Seaforth, Ontario, and later came to Muskoka, married Leah Duke of Port Carling, and settled near Skeleton Bay on Lake Rosseau. He may have leased the mills at Dee Bank for a time, but in 1885 he acquired the Hutcheson mill at the river mouth and was soon processing thousands of logs floated down from Three Mile Lake or towed in by his little tug, the *Dee*, which was later replaced by the *Gypsy*, a former yacht from Minett. (Probably the tugs were also used to take scowloads of sawn lumber to various customers around the lakes.) About sixteen men were needed to staff the mill, and quarters were provided for them. Clark also did custom work for the local people. To enlarge the millpond on the river above the mill, and to regulate the water flows, he built a new dam, and engaged William Skinner of Windermere to haul some of the rocks for it. The falls have since been known as Clark's Falls.

If the village of Windermere was doing well at this time, the same cannot be said for its neighbour at Dee Bank. Relatively little is known about the fortunes of the Dee mills today. The gristmill and the Barber tannery were still operating as late as 1890, but the former was destroyed by fire at an unknown date, and by 1895 the Shannons lost the property following a mortgage foreclosure; some of the family moved for a time to Port Carling, where Peter Shannon became the lockmaster. In 1903 James Barber sold the tannery property to one of his relatives for a mere pittance — which probably means that the tannery had ceased to exist by then. That same year the post office was closed.

The sawmill lasted longer. At the end of 1895 it passed to August Briese, a German settler-entrepreneur who already owned a mill and a steamboat on Skeleton Lake. Briese ran the Dee mill with success, and was progressive enough to insist that his employees buy insurance from the Independent Order of Foresters in the event of death or accidents on the job — as tragically befell Earl Duboise, a log-driver who was knocked off a pier above the Dee River falls during the spring drive of 1899, swept into the spillway, and drowned amid the logs in the millpond. The Briese family settled in a house below the old school, and also ran the farm now owned by Murray Taylor of Windermere, west of the modern bridge; the barn still stands, but not the sawmill. According to a newspaper clipping, the Brieses ran the mill for ten years (until approximately 1906), but then it went up in flames and was never rebuilt. (The same fate overtook the Briese mills at Ullswater.) Forestry was now dying out around the Muskoka Lakes, and in 1911 August Briese sold the millsite property to his son Albert (who was later to become reeve of Watt) and retired to his home at Ullswater, where he died in 1921. The Dee Bank schoolhouse was closed in 1913 and converted into a residence; later still it became a school again (S. S. No. 5, Watt). Today it is being restored as a private home.

In short, Dee Bank Village died with the mills. Apparently the employees could not purchase the houses they lived in, and consequently had little incentive to stay. By about 1910 there was little left. Old-timers still recall the old steel shafts and rusting machinery from the sawmill, lying at the foot of the falls, along with the abandoned grindstones from the gristmill. Around 1939 all of the pieces were sold for scrap, and today there is not a trace of the little industrial complex built by the Shannons. Only a few farms remain, and today it is hard to imagine that this quiet spot was once such a hive of activity. Lately there has been a revival of sorts: the road from the river to Ullswater has officially been named the Dee Bank Road, and since 1970 a cottage and residential subdivision has been opened along the Strathdee Road near the southwest corner of Three Mile Lake. Although set at a different location, the new development is still called Dee Bank Village.

Was the decline of the old Dee Bank a direct result of the rise of Windermere? To some extent, yes: the church and school both deserted the former for the latter, and a number of families did the same. Dee Bank Village was a product of the Muskoka farms and forests, and declined when the mills disappeared. Windermere was a child of steamboating and the resort industry, which was rising to undreamed-of heights, as the advent of the Laurier era ushered in a period of unprecedented prosperity in Canada — and to the regions close to the Muskoka Lakes.

Windermere House, ca. 1898, before the front section was lengthened.

• CHAPTER 2 •

THE GLORIOUS YEARS (1896–1929)

BY 1896 A NEW ERA was beginning in Canadian history. The Liberals under Wilfrid Laurier were swept into power in Ottawa, ending nearly two decades of increasingly moribund Conservative rule and ushering in one of the most prosperous intervals in Canadian history. Thousands of new settlers were pouring into the West, while the mills and factories of the East rushed to meet their needs. In Muskoka the pioneer period was definitely over, and the tourist industry — gradually perceived to be a godsend — was rapidly replacing lumbering as the mainstay of the local economy.

The resorts were getting distinctly fancier and more opulent. Many could now offer tennis and shuffleboard courts to keep the guests amused. Several had a private steam yacht available. Some were using acetylene gas for lighting, and producing it themselves. A few were even creating septic drainage fields, as people gradually became more sensitive about water pollution; even so, the "summer complaint" caused by tainted water still persisted into the 1930s. The big hotels were now becoming very "fashionable," reflecting the social class cleavages then so strong in the cities: interaction between tourists and local people became more and more distant. Guests now disembarked from the lake steamers in style, bringing swarms of servants to look after them, and nannies to look after the children. (The servants always occupied separate quarters, always distinctly inferior to those of their employers.) Invariably guests would also bring huge trunks containing their belongings, since everyone expected to stay at least a month, if not the whole season. (Husbands were not always so lucky, and might have had to limit their time to weekends.)

Windermere House was definitely one of the really "big" hotels. It was a constant struggle for Thomas Aitken and his family to keep finding new ways to keep it abreast of the latest trends. In 1902-03 they built another major extension to the front of the building at the north end, increasing the total area to 32,000 square feet, and added a second tower; this made room for forty new bedrooms, while the frontage was increased to about 200 feet. The dining and reception rooms were also enlarged. About this time kerosene lanterns gave way to acetylene, which was considered a vast improvement. A white, wooden picket fence decorated the road to the wharf, but by 1908 it had been rebuilt of stone. Windermere House could now take two hundred guests, at rates of $1.50 per day or $7 to $9 per week. (This might sound extremely cheap by today's standards, but one dollar a day was still the average wage at the turn of the century.) A brochure published in 1904 describes the great hotel as follows:

"Windermere House, at Windermere, on Lake Rosseau, is another favourite stopping-place [for the lake steamers], and one of the largest hotels on the chain of lakes. It is situated on a high bluff close to the water's edge, and within a minute or two from the steamer wharf. The great verandah space and double balconies which surround this house, measure over one eighth of a mile . . . In close proximity to Windermere are several lakes, among which are Skeleton and Trout lakes, where black bass and salmon trout are plentiful . . . well-stocked stores near by supply all [additional] requirements of the guests. There are two churches, Methodist and Presbyterian, near the hotel. The rooms of the Windermere are high and roomy, and the hallways wide, thus securing a cool house at all times. The sanitary arrangements and drainage have recently been entirely remodelled according to modern requirements. There is a new concert hall, dancing, music, lawn-tennis, bowling, bathing on a good sand beach, boating, fishing etc., furnish abundant amusement. The rates are $2.00 per day, $9.00 and $12.00 per week. Mails every day. Thomas Aitken, proprietor."

The neighbouring resorts were not doing badly either. The Fife House was taking eighty guests by 1903, at rates of $1.25 per day or $7 per week. It was a very relaxed place, and in 1901 an advertisement concisely observed that it featured "nice sandy beach, safe in all parts, at the door; beautifully shaded by fine grove; best spring water; good boating and driving; table the specialty of the house; first-class piano and best furnished rooms." The Fifes sometimes arranged evening hayrides for their guests, who would invariably return in good spirits, tossing hay at one another and shouting the Fife House yell — to the

HOTEL STAFF, WINDERMERE HOUSE, AUGUST 1906. WILLIAM AND ANNIE AITKEN WITH DOG (LOWER RIGHT). (FLORENCE AITKEN)

occasional discomfiture of Windermere House guests who were trying to sleep! In 1907 plumbing was installed at the Fife House, using hot air engines to pump the water; four years later, gasoline engines were substituted until the advent of electricity in 1930.

In the summer of 1900 the village was the scene of another huge regatta. Boats were everywhere, bringing in the local cottagers, while hundreds more spectators arrived aboard the elegant white steamers of the Navigation Company. The local people trooped in by land. Corsetted ladies in laces and long dresses and wide-brimmed hats mingled with gentlemen with handlebar mustaches and city dudes sporting straw hats, tailored suits, starched collars, and button boots. Small children scampered underfoot, and here and there one might spot the ships' officers in their immaculate blue uniforms, white caps, and gold braid, shouting orders amid the hubbub. There were canoe and rowboat races, wherein the paddlers sometimes had to use their bare hands, plus canoe-tilting and log-burling contests by the lumberjacks, while the onlookers ooohed and aaahed and cheered their favourites. A special feature was the log race, which required a log to be paddled a distance of 100 feet using only a pike pole; Tom Clark, the sawmill owner, usually won. The festivities were climaxed by an evening dance at the hotels. Almost the only thing to mar the season were reports of a diphtheria epidemic around Ullswater and Dee Bank, but fortunately there were few cases in Windermere.

Amidst all this the residents at Windermere (who numbered about 130 in 1899) tried to carry on with their lives and meet the needs of the tourists. Around 1896 Thomas Johnston of Port Carling (from the famous family of boatbuilders) took over the Windermere boat livery, renting and selling boats from a boathouse located on the breakwater pier, adjacent to the beach. An ice-cream shop and summer store were located nearby. During this period John Insley, usually known as Jack, opened a blacksmith shop. In 1902 Thomas Clark left Windermere to take up a new life as a farmer near New Liskeard; the following year the family lost their sawmill to Edward Jordan, a merchant from Rosseau, in default of a mortgage payment, and for a time the mill was shut down. However, in 1913 Thomas Henry Clark, one of the sons, managed to buy it back. The plant was reopened and resumed cutting until 1929.

Until 1896 the village had no store, except the small one run by Mrs. Inglis, but around that time Perry Prosser, whose family lived near Brackenrig, moved in and built a grocery store across the street from Windermere House; the family lived upstairs. Prosser stayed only briefly, then relinquished the store to his brother Frank, who had previously been known as a horse trader. Frank Prosser carried on, and also bought a steamboat, the *Maple Leaf* (8 tons), in 1900, which he perhaps intended to use for peddling provisions, but little came of it. He ran the store for several years, but the villagers were seemingly a bit wary of him. They considered him a rather rough, unsavoury character, and it is said that when his daughter came down with diphtheria in the early summer of 1900 Prosser locked her up in her room and refused to summon help, fearing diminished profits if the secret got out. It did nonetheless and the store was quarantined, while the proprietor loudly lamented his losses. In 1904 Prosser's wife died, and sometime later he left the area. His store was sold in 1909 to Richard John Lance of Beatrice, who carried on with it until about 1912, when it was sold to William Aitken, who relinquished his occupation as a farmer and leased the family farm to a tenant. William moved the telegraph office and post office into the store and proceeded to run them both, assisted by his wife, Annie. If the mail arrived late, as sometimes happened during the winters, the store remained open until the letters had been sorted. In 1920 Aitken officially became the postmaster, and held the position until April 1949.

ANNIE FORGE AITKEN AND WILLIAM AITKEN. (FLORENCE AITKEN)

The store was a country general store: it sold everything from overalls and socks to biscuits, dishes, hardware and pipe fittings — and ice, which was harvested from the lake during the winters. The goods were bought from city salesmen. During the 1920s it became the first place in Windermere to sell gasoline. The pumps were initially set up on the breakwater, close to the bay but not close enough for the hoses to reach the boats — with the result that the vendors had to carry the gasoline in cans! It is said that Willie Aitken was such a good-natured sort that he never pressed his customers to pay, but despite this he remained in business for about eighteen years. In 1912 David Fife Junior sold an adjacent plot of land with a building on it to his ambitious son Stuart, who proceeded to open a store, but the popular young man overexerted himself while moving drums of coal oil in July of 1913, sustained a ruptured appendix, and died for lack of a surgeon. He was just twenty-two. The Fife store was then taken over by William Aitken, who used it for the storage of paint and supplies; much later it would house the Windermere Dairy.

By the turn of the century the village was about to acquire yet another church, this one largely a creation of the local cottagers. Hitherto, the nearest Anglican church was St. Thomas's in Ullswater, opened around 1882. However, as early as 1889 the Reverend Charles Mockridge, rector of Christ Church Cathedral at Hamilton, bought property from the Forges for a summer home, and was soon holding services on his front porch; they were later transferred to the Mechanics' Institute building. Steadily he formed the conviction that there must be an Anglican church in Windermere. In 1900 a plot of land was purchased behind Windermere House for twenty-five dollars, and gradually a little frame summer church was raised. Some of the local people helped out, while much of the work was done by Mockridge himself, aided by his four sons (all of whom were ultimately ordained). Charles Cox of Bracebridge built the pews, altar, and font and arranged the shingling, while the lectern was made by the cottager William Fairclough of Hamilton. The interior of the church is beautifully panelled with cedar, and decorated with unique wood designs burned into them by two American cottagers from Richmond, Virginia, both pyrographic experts. By 1904 it was completed. Christ Church Anglican is like a tiny spiritual oasis, and is open every season from May to October. In later years Mr. Britton Michael Osler, whose cottage stood on part of the old Forge farm, donated an organ to the church in memory of Mockridge.

In October 1911 the Windermere Women's Institute was founded, on the initiative of Mrs. Herman Goltz of Bardsville. Over the years it has made sterling contributions to many worthy causes, including providing for home economics classes for young women, making contributions to charity and community improvements, helping victims of fire, buying equipment for hospitals, providing benches and life buoys at the village wharf, and countless other things. During the two world wars the women knit socks and scarfs for the troops, made jackets for minesweeper crews, and assembled aid packages. Around 1931 the Institute began compiling records of local history, and thus saved much village lore that would otherwise have been lost. Mrs. Elizabeth Forge, wife of Francis, was the first president.

Around the same time, Windermere also got its own school. Hitherto, all the children had had to walk to the little, brick schoolhouse at Dee Bank, for which William Aitken, James Bogart and David Fife Junior served as trustees. But Dee Bank was declining and Windermere was growing, and in 1912 a meeting was held to move No. 5 Watt into Windermere. Thomas Huggard, at this time the owner of the Thomas Fife farm, agreed to sell an acre of land at the edge of the village for one hundred dollars for the purpose. The new brick school was built by the Waltenbury brothers of Bracebridge, while George Dawson and James Fife did the carpentry. It was opened in 1913, under the direction of Miss Olive Dickinson. The school itself was a one-room building, with a porch in front and a wooden annex at the rear, containing a woodshed and two toilets. It never had a bell. A spring near the Beech Ridge Hill furnished drinking water, but in later years a well was sunk. Later still a basement was added, plus chemical toilets. A furnace replaced the box stove, and in 1930 it was electrified. The school enrollment swelled to fifty or sixty students of all ages, who sometimes turned it into a scene from bedlam. (Perhaps for this reason few teachers stayed long.)

MR. AND MRS. IRENAEUS HOUGH IN THE LOBBY OF MAPLE LEAF HOUSE. (THE BALDWINS)

Still the influx of summer people grew, and soon the resorts at Windermere had no room for expansion. The result was that more resorts appeared. One was opened by Irenaeus Hough, who had come to Canada in 1871. He settled in Muskoka, married Ella "Nellie" Clark in 1895 (one of the eleven children of Thomas, the sawmill owner), and built the original Morinus House on the northwest side of Lake Rosseau. In the meantime he also purchased land from Thomas Aitken, built a cottage, and took in boarders arriving on the steamers. In 1901 Hough decided to go into tourism in a big way and built the Maple Leaf House, on the little bay immediately north of Paton Point. The new hotel was surrounded by woodlands and meadows, and offered a safe, sandy beach, and a baseball diamond, with a large farm and vegetable garden. By 1903 it was taking thirty-five guests. Mr. Hough also provided his own wharf for the Navigation Company steamers, complete with a canopy for shelter, and in 1904 he spruced up the hotel by adding a new ballroom with a large fireplace.

In 1905 the new hotel suffered a major setback. One chilly day Mr. Hough's five-year-old son, Ivan, decided to build a fire under the front porch of the hotel "to keep his little dog warm" and in the process burned down the entire building! Mr. Hough returned from Bracebridge that evening to find nothing but a vast heap of glowing cinders. However, he accepted the terrified child's report quite calmly, despite the fact that the hotel was uninsured, and simply resolved to build it anew. By 1906 a new Maple Leaf House had arisen on the same site, and by 1916 it had expanded to take sixty patrons. It was a very informal place, where the guests enjoyed such "plebeian" activities as baseball games, dancing to phonograph music, or singalongs accompanied by a banjo. "Rene" Hough was a big, handsome, eccentric man who loved sports, especially skating, canoeing, and ball games. For a time he was also a justice of the peace and an avid drummer in the Bracebridge Orange parades, but a businessman he was not, since he never bothered to keep systematic records.

(BEVERLEY HEYD)

This was the heyday of hotel building, and already two more resorts had appeared a little north of Windermere. One was King's Park, which was located on a delightful little bay with a sandy beach, about two miles north of the village. The founder, Charles Gerrard King, purchased Lot 32, Concession X in 1889 and proceeded to develop a small dairy farm. His decision to turn his farmhouse into a resort probably came later, but by 1903 King's Park House was well established, with gas lighting and its own steamboat wharf. It offered fine bathing, fishing, and canoeing, separate cottages, and tennis courts amid a quiet setting for up to seventy-five guests at rates of $1.25 per day or $6 to $8 per week. Charles King has been described as a rather stuffy Englishman, but his resort was quite successful, and remained open for over half a century.

A greater establishment was Rostrevor Lodge, which was built a little further north in 1896. Its owner, Arthur Dinsmore, was born at Rostrevor, in County Down, Ireland, in 1839. The family immigrated to Toronto in 1869, and two years later moved to Bracebridge, and thence to Lake Rosseau in 1874. Mr. Dinsmore spent the next five years clearing some fifteen acres for a farm; his brother Fred located nearby, north of Clark's Pond. The Dinsmores also engaged in logging for a time until they, too, sensed the new trend to tourism. In 1896 Arthur demolished his original home and erected a large two-storey building with verandahs and a red mansard roof, which he named after his birthplace. It commanded a natural, sandy beach about 1,500 feet long — easily the finest on

Lake Rosseau — and naturally it also had a long steamboat wharf. A summer post office soon followed. Rostrevor Lodge was initially a sportsmen's haven, frequented mainly by hunters and fishermen, and its flavour was distinctly masculine. As of 1903 Mr. Dinsmore was taking thirty-five guests, but this figure jumped to sixty by 1906 and one hundred by 1916. In his last years Arthur Dinsmore suffered a disabling stroke which left him weak and paralyzed, and on October 7, 1912, he died at his beloved Rostrevor, but the lodge carried on in the family for many more years.

Another once-famous resort that was to play a major role in the life of Windermere was Waskada Lodge, which was built diagonally opposite the village on a lofty headland on the northeast corner of Tobin Island. The site, once owned by William Groom (who married May Tobin), was purchased by Frank S. Hurlburt of Toronto, who opened the Waskada in 1906. The new hotel was a lofty, sprawling three-storey building with sufficient accommodation for 110 guests. It had hexagonal towers and a dark-red roof and matching boathouses. The property comprised 218 acres and included more than two miles of shoreline. It featured nature trails, horseback riding, tennis courts, bowling greens, croquet grounds, badminton courts, and boating, besides campfires, card games and dancing in the evenings. In 1912 Hurlburt sold the hotel to W. J. Rice, also from Toronto. Rice kept the resort until 1921.

FORGE FAMILY, WINDERMERE. FRANCIS FORGE, THE PATRIARCH, STANDS FOURTH FROM THE LEFT IN THE BACK ROW. HENRY AND EDITH (FORGE) LONGHURST ARE SEATED, CENTRE. WILLIAM AITKEN, FRONT LEFT, HOLDING HIS BABY DAUGHTER, IRENE.

(FLORENCE AITKEN)

By 1909 the five resorts of Windermere (excluding Waskada) could take about 465 guests — which meant that the summer people often outnumbered the locals by more than four to one. (For a short time there was even a sixth facility, known as Momiji Farm, which in 1916 was offering accommodations for fifteen people, but unfortunately no one today seems to remember where this property was.) By 1908 the Navigation Company was also near its zenith, using nine steamers to bring in the crowds from Muskoka Wharf or Lake Joseph Station, and for the first time the deep-throated whistle of the *Sagamo* was heard daily at Windermere. Old-timers still recall watching deck hands unloading huge heaps of freight and baggage onto horse-drawn wagons bound for the stores and hotels; included were piled-up wooden boxes full of loaves of fresh bread from Bracebridge. By the same token large consignments of milk, cream, and lamb cuts from the local farms were loaded aboard the *Sagamo* to be taken to the resorts at Minett. Every summer the village became incredibly animated, especially as most of the villagers worked directly or indirectly for the tourists. At season's end and throughout the long cold siege of winter, the community grew quiet again, carrying on with chopping wood, cutting ice, tapping maple trees, attending church or school, doing chores, and preparing for the next tourist season.

In 1913 there was a brief panic on the stock markets, and suddenly the chatty news from the Muskoka resorts in the Toronto newspapers collapsed. Then the First World War broke out, and as its grim realities began to sink in the resort scene became more and more subdued. Men became scarce, and many commodities were rationed. As a result some of the hotels had to cut back their services or take fewer guests. But the setback proved temporary, and when the armistice of 1918 proved to be truly the end of the war, Windermere celebrated the return of peace with another mammoth regatta. By 1921 things seemed more or less normal again.

But there were differences. Harrows and harvesters were replacing scythes and hoes on the farms. Horseless carriages were proliferating rapidly in the cities, and now and then the occasional motorcar could be seen bumping its way over the dusty roads as far north as Muskoka. Steam launches were giving way rapidly to gas-powered motorboats, which, aided by the rapid evolution of the internal-combustion engine during the war, were soon able to race about at amazing speeds of twenty, thirty or even forty miles per hour. Speedboat racing, fuelled by daredevil spirits and cheap gasoline, became a popular pastime on Lake Rosseau. One result of all this was the establishment of a marina at Windermere. Nathaniel "Dan" Bogart, a son of Jake, was the first to do this, erecting his boathouses on part of the government road allowance along the shore next to the village wharf, while his wife ran a small restaurant there. In later years their son Wyman took it over, assisted by his wife, Reta. During the 1930s it went to Arthur Cuff of Renfrew.

A number of prominent new cottagers moved in during this period, including the lawyer Britton Osler of the firm of Osler, Hoskin, and Harcourt in Toronto, who settled next to Eaton Point, where he had once pitched his tent. Osler was a relative of the famous Dr. William Osler and would later assist with the incorporation of Windermere. Albert Matthews, a stockbroker, purchased property on Eaton Point in 1921 for $8,500. He was to later become lieutenant-governor of Ontario, and today the local access road around the beach at Windermere Bay still bears his name. Another new cottager was the amiable C. L. Burton, who was building up Simpson's Department Store in Toronto, in competition with Eaton's. Another was Wilfred P. Western, a curmudgeonly old English gentleman whose cottage stood on Portage Bay. Still another was the famous Canadian Air Force ace William "Billy" Bishop, who made aviation history by shooting down seventy-two German aircraft during the First World War. Bishop married a granddaughter of Timothy Eaton, and with fellow ace Colonel Billy Barker ran a seaplane service between Toronto and the Royal Muskoka Hotel during those years. (It is regrettable that some old-timers at Windermere remember Colonel Bishop as a nuisance who often appeared "lit"; he was quite pleasant when sober.) Other celebrities included Sir Albert and Lady Gooderham of Toronto and North Bohemia Island; financial wizard and Nobel Peace Prize winner, Professor George Stigler of Chicago University; Gary Whiteside, head of the Canada Farm Loan Board; and Edward Y. Eaton, son of Timothy, whose fine property on Rockledge Point still stands. If anything, the villagers seemed to find the cottagers nicer than the hotel guests, who seemed more aloof.

After the war the flavour of the resorts began to change: the well-to-do were growing tired of the stiff, formal garb that epitomized the rigid propriety of their daily lives and were discarding starched collars and constricting corsets for looser, more casual clothes that did not differ substantially from those of working people. Their daughters wore shorter skirts, bobbed their hair, and began smoking cigarettes. Swimsuits grew scantier, and ceased to look like diving suits. The era of the Roaring Twenties had arrived.

With the return of good times came yet another resort at Windermere. In September 1920 a natty, fussy English painter named Frederick William Newton, who sometimes worked at Windermere House and Llanllar, purchased a property along the modern Fife Road, a little north of the Maple Leaf House, and built a large green-and-white three-storey summer hotel that he named the Newtonia. It stood east of the road and was a very expensive, formal place featuring a croquet field. It had no direct access to the water, although Maple Leaf Bay was immediately adjacent. "Daddy" Newton ran the Newtonia for just two years and apparently could not make it pay. By the fall of 1923 he went bankrupt and sold the property to his neighbour,

FIFE HOUSE, CA. 1920.

George Bunn, for eight thousand dollars. Bunn held the property until the spring of 1927, when, after a convoluted court case, the hotel was awarded to Ralph J. Cutten, a Toronto stockbroker and a brother of Arthur Cutten, the "wheat king" of Chicago. Cutten had the building moved in sections across the road to Maple Leaf Bay, using rollers and winches. It became a sort of private flophouse where he and his buddies could drink or hold wild parties. It was later purchased by C. Lloyd Smith, a businessman from Hamilton, who turned it into the Silver Birches resort. The original site was sold to the Maple Leaf House for fifteen thousand dollars.

The old founding settlers and resort owners were gradually going to their rewards. David Fife Senior died in 1914. When Elizabeth Forge died in 1928 at the age of eighty-two, practically all of Windermere united in presenting floral tributes; since the village has no cemeteries, she was buried at Ullswater. She and her aging husband, Francis, who had finally relinquished both his farm and his boat, moved into a brick house built in 1900 in the village proper; Timothy Eaton furnished it for them. The farm went briefly to Forge's son Edward, who soon married a local girl and went west. It was then sold to Henry Longhurst, one of the sons of Albert Longhurst of Ufford. Henry had recently returned from Saskatchewan with the avowed intention of marrying Edith Forge, one of Francis's daughters, whom he had met five years earlier while working at Windermere House. He accomplished this aim in 1907, fixed up the farm, and eventually purchased a herd of Holstein cattle to supply dairy products. From 1907 to 1915 he ran his own supply-boat service, peddling eggs, vegetables, veal, and fresh-cut lamb from a rowboat until he could finish paying for his new house. (His father-in-law lent a hand by introducing Henry to his old customers.) Mr. Forge himself lingered on as one of Windermere's most respected citizens, spending his last few years in the living quarters of the Aitken store until his death on January 2, 1930, at the age of ninety-one. The Forge home in Windermere went to his daughter Annie, who had married William Aitken; it was rented to the contractor Milton Goltz for eleven years and then became the home of Annie's son Fred.

In his last years Thomas Aitken stopped by every day for a chat with Francis Forge, until Aitken himself died, on December 23, 1919, at the age of eighty-seven, having lived to see his great hotel, and indeed the entire village, arise from literally nothing, largely thanks to his efforts. He was buried at Ufford. His wife, Elizabeth, outlived him by nearly seventeen years and long remained a presence at Windermere House. The hotel passed to their son Leslie, then thirty, and his wife, Maude Dakar, a pianist from Cleveland.

David Fife Junior left in 1914. After running the Fife House successfully for twenty-five years, he finally grew tired of it. His devoted wife, always the mainstay of his life, passed away in 1910, to be followed by his eldest daughter the following year, and his son Stuart in 1913. Many of his other children had already moved elsewhere, or would soon do so. Amidst all this David Fife decided to leave as well. He sold his farm to Frederick Briese for $3,700, and the hotel to Thomas M. Johnston, who was already running the boat livery, and moved with his youngest son to Talbotville, where he operated a gristmill for a time. In 1929 he died of a heart attack at age seventy-two; his body was brought back to the Fife House prior to burial at Ullswater. Thus Windermere lost another of its most esteemed citizens, a quiet, studious man devoted to his church and family, and never known to refuse anyone help. It is said that he even acted as the unofficial village doctor, taking instructions from a qualified physician in Bracebridge by telephone.

John Inglis died suddenly in 1909 of a heart attack, but his widow, Nellie, carried on with Ingleside House for another twenty-two years. Old-timers still vaguely recall the old lady, seldom seen but always watching by the light of a lantern from the front room of her house. In 1923 Charles King died, leaving King's Park to his daughter Barbara Agnes, who ran it successfully for another sixteen years. She sometimes touted her resort as "the coolest and pleasantest place in Muskoka." It was a lively, informal place, noted especially for sailing and water sports.

Some of the other resorts were changing owners during this time. In 1921 Major Leonard T. Trump and his brother, Captain Ernest Trump, purchased Rostrevor Lodge (which may have languished following the death of Arthur Dinsmore) and turned it into a pleasant family resort, which they operated with characteristic English grace. Florence Broley of Ivy, Ontario, who worked for the Trumps for three seasons before marrying Fred Aitken, found her employers congenial, well-bred, friendly people who tended to attract wealthy guests.

In the village itself there were a few new developments. Henry Longhurst, hitherto a farmer, had gone into the building trade and helped build or renovate several cottages; he also did caretaking work for the Eatons and the Oslers, who bought land from him in 1922. Thomas Huggard, who had moved into the village from his farm at Dee Bank in 1907, opened a little summer store in his house to sell ice cream, candies, and the like, opposite the Methodist church. Burton (Bert) Insley took over his father's blacksmith shop or established his own, east of the modern Taylor store, charging seventy cents to shoe a horse. He also became a maintenance man at Windermere House before landing a winter job at Simpson's Department Store in Toronto (thanks to C. L. Burton, who arranged many such positions for local people).

Perhaps the most obvious development during this period was the new golf course. It was originally a nine-hole course, built mostly on Thomas Aitken's old farm (though part of it once belonged to Thomas Huggard). It was financed by a consortium of well-to-do cottagers who formed the Windermere Golf and Country Club in 1919; Leslie Aitken had shares in it. The course was laid out by George Cummings of Toronto and officially opened on August 4, 1920, before several hundred spectators. James Cooper Mason, general manager of the Home Bank of Canada, became the first president, and amongst the shareholders were Toronto financiers E. R. Wood and G. H. Gundy, publisher Hugh C. MacLean, Dr. C. M. Hincks, Mrs. Timothy Eaton and Britton Osler. The fees were then just ten dollars per season. It has since been expanded into an eighteen-hole championship course, covering 124 acres; part of the Windermere Road, which originally entered the village in front of the school, had to be relocated further east to make room for it. Needless to say, it is patronized by the guests at all the resorts. Verena Newton, a daughter of Fred, was an avid golfer and became Ontario's first female pro. A clubhouse was built in 1920, and a Mr. Burrows was hired as the first pro, later to be followed by Hugh Logan, a soft-spoken, pipe-smoking little Scotsman from Toronto, who served for about twenty-five years. Logan's big, husky son Hugh Junior succeeded him. In 1960 James MacLeod, a pro from Glasgow, Scotland and Bermuda, became the general manager. Under his direction the clubhouse was enlarged, several fairways lengthened and various ponds added to improve drainage and increase the hazards! Tennis courts were also built, as well as a gift and coffee shop at the clubhouse. William Bunn of Windermere acted as superintendent and was later succeeded by his son Elmer. It is thanks largely to them that the course has been kept in such excellent shape. One of the side effects of the golf course is that it squeezes and constrains the village against the lake, leaving little room for new homes.

A less tangible development during those years was the appearance of the Epworth League of the Methodist Church, which had been holding temperance rallies at Grimsby, Ontario, as early as 1859. The league, whose aim was to promote Protestant values and morals (along with providing some recreation and education), held its first week-long Muskoka Summer School at Windermere House in the summer of 1916. It was organized by the Reverend Charles Sinclair Applegath, a Methodist minister then in charge of a church in Galt (Cambridge), at a time when morality seemed to have been undermined by doubt and debased by the war and the "flapper mentality" of the 1920s. The Windermere gathering proved so successful that a second one was held in 1917 at the Elgin House on Lake Joseph, where the grounds were more spacious. Applegath, however, soon found the Epworth League too rigid, structured, and evangelical for his liking. He wanted to nourish the body and mind as well as the spirit, and took for granted that Christian teachings must keep abreast of the latest advances in scientific knowledge. As a result, he switched to the format of the Chautauqua, an American organization that had held its first meetings at Lake Chautauqua, New York, in 1874. Unlike the Epworth League, the Chautauqua was very liberal and nonsectarian, and attracted highly qualified speakers and lecturers.

It was a problem, however, to launch his new idea. In 1920 Applegath, who had been taking young Epworth Leaguers on camping trips in the Windermere area, bought a cottage on adjacent Tobin Island. He soon found out that Waskada Lodge was itself for sale. Business there had been depressed by the war, which made mortgage payments more and more difficult, and worse, Sidney Rice, the proprietor's son, had been killed overseas in 1916. Mr. Rice then gave up the effort, and the property was left to languish. To Charles Applegath it seemed the perfect, secluded natural setting for the new chautauqua-type assemblies he was planning. He promptly gathered together a group of eighteen investors, formed the Canadian Chautauqua Institution, sold shares, bought the property, and renamed it the Epworth Inn. The rather dilapidated buildings were upgraded and repainted, and a number of cottage lots were sold off to raise more money. On July 1, 1921, the Chautauqua Institution was in business, although it was never officially connected with the American Chautauqua or the various travelling chautauquas then trying to bring culture and entertainment to many small Canadian towns.

The Muskoka Assemblies at Epworth Inn featured a delightful mixture of lectures, seminars, debates, discussion groups, historical re-enactments, sports, games, boating, swimming, campfires, costume parties, and dancing, always launched with morning prayer and meditations. Soon its activities were expanded to offer courses in art, astronomy, music, literature, and drama. Some gatherings attracted up to two hundred participants. Clergymen and college professors taught subjects as varied as foreign cultures, comparative religion, and theosophy. All sorts of interesting people attended from time to time, including cartoonist John Wilson Bengough, publisher Lorne Pierce, noted author Jules Tremblay, novelists R. E. Knowles, Sir Gilbert Parker and Margaret Marshall Saunders, and poets such as Sir Charles G. D. Roberts and his son Lloyd, Bliss Carman, E. J. Pratt, Dorothy Livesay and Wilson MacDonald, thus turning Epworth Inn into a cultural and intellectual mecca. Some of these literati also gave readings and lectures at the adjacent resorts. For eleven seasons the chautauqua was a prominent and beneficent influence around Lake Rosseau, until changing times and economics forced it to disband.

Shortly after the war, the feeling grew that Windermere should incorporate itself as a separate village. The villagers wanted hydro-electric power and paved streets, and began to feel that their interests were being ignored by the Township of Watt. These sentiments were fanned by Henry Longhurst, who was now running the Forge farm and acting as a building contractor. With legal assistance and some coaching from Britton Osler and his colleagues, and a little moral support from George W. Ecclestone, the local MPP, Mr. Longhurst personally took his petition to Queen's Park in 1924 and presented it to the Private Bills Committee. The Township of Watt bitterly opposed it and engaged two lawyers to argue that Windermere was much too small to become an incorporated village, and that it was never likely to get any bigger. But the measure passed nonetheless, seventy-one to zero, and on April 17, 1924, Windermere became the smallest incorporated village in Ontario — at least in population! Its boundaries extended north as far as Clark's Pond and the Dee River, south to the Forge (Longhurst) farm on Portage Bay, and east to the Rostrevor Road and the Dawson Road to the southeast. It also encompassed Florence and Wellesley Islands. At the first council meeting, held in the village school, Henry Longhurst was elected reeve, a position he was to hold for forty years. The first four councillors were Leslie Aitken, Thomas Huggard, Fred Newton and Arthur Fife; none were paid. Charles Roper became the first clerk, to be followed by Fred Aitken, James Donaldson (who worked at Llanllar), and finally (around 1962) Edwin A. Paullette, who by then was running the village store.

Initially the new council had nary a cent to its name, but it immediately began attending to such priorities as forming its own school board, repairing the streets, and beautifying the community. Another urgent priority was to get rid of some of the old wharves and boathouses on the bay, which were becoming unsightly and dangerous. A problem surfaced when it was discovered that Thomas Huggard had a quitclaim deed on some of the Ditchburn boathouses, but Longhurst persuaded him to sell his claim for twenty-five dollars; Huggard also agreed to demolish the boathouses within two months. Other improvements came gradually as finances allowed, though the roads were not paved until the late 1940s. The school, which was grossly overcrowded, was taken over, and restricted to village children; all the rest had to go to the reopened Dee Bank school, much to the irritation of some of their families. Around 1928 a grade nine class was introduced, but for some time it was difficult for students to get any further secondary education unless they could arrange to board at Bracebridge. The Windermere school served until November 4, 1966, when a new consolidated public school was built at Ullswater.

Meanwhile new residents were moving into Windermere, many of whom provided useful services. In 1924 Thomas Edgar Fraser purchased a lot close to the Newtonia from his father and opened a

R.M.S. *Sagamo* CALLS AT WINDERMERE, CA. 1926. (IRENE WASLEY DICKSON)

barbershop next to the modern Taylor store; later he rented space in William Aitken's store across from Windermere House, and later still worked out of his home. It was a summer service only; in winters Mr. Fraser worked in Huntsville and Bracebridge. In 1927 Milton Goltz, a building contractor from Bardsville, moved in and began a very successful career building and maintaining cottages. Much later he was elected village reeve and provided progressive leadership. Initially he was friendly with Henry Longhurst, but unfortunately the two men soon fell out (perhaps because both were engaged in the contracting business) and would scarcely speak to one another. It proved the longest and bitterest feud in the history of Windermere, a place normally noted for its tranquility. When the Second World War broke out, Longhurst reminded everyone that Goltz was a German, but this stunt backfired and many of Longhurst's customers deserted to Goltz.

Another innovation was the formation of a transport service. Most freight consignments had traditionally arrived by steamer, but in 1924 Fred Aitken, a son of William, obtained a licence from the Board of Transport to haul merchandise of all sorts, including lumber, furniture, feed, seed, and foodstuffs for a growing list of customers between Windermere and Bracebridge. Soon the Aitken Transport truck left every morning at five o'clock to meet the trains at Bracebridge station to collect consignments of meat from Schneider's and Canada Packers, which were unloaded onto wagons and then onto the trucks. There was often a lot of confusion during sorting, but it was vitally important to avoid mix-ups and to get everything loaded in the proper order, with the first deliveries going on last for ease of unloading. It was not uncommon to find waybills with the instructions "Transfer to Aitken at Windermere"!

The warm seasons were — and are — the busy times at Windermere, in that most of the local people earn their livelihoods by catering to cottagers, running stores, building docks and cottages, opening and closing them in the spring and fall, and servicing boats. (Few village residents own their own boats, and in any case docking space is limited.) As a result the villagers had little time for summer recreation, beyond the occasional swim or game of golf. Winter was the season for getting caught up on chores around the house or farm. Most villagers now had warm homes and ample stoves and fireplaces to keep them so. Children played softball in the summers and went tobogganing down the local hills in winter, or skated on Paton Bay — or later at a rink at Fred Aitken's home because the lake ice was prone to split and heave and flood. The men also formed a hockey team (sometimes known as the Windermere Wildcats) that would play the Three Mile Lake Wolves on the local rink. Sometimes they might also play at Port Carling, Huntsville, Port Sydney, Allensville, or Milford Bay if the roads were passable, using old magazines tucked inside their socks as shinguards. The men sometimes went curling at Bracebridge, and in November there was always the fall deer hunt. The ladies would frequently meet for afternoon or evening teas at their neighbours' homes, where they could knit and chitchat and get caught up on all the latest news. A few families even had radios, which gave them an ear to the outside world, and there was always the weekly newspaper and the triweekly mail. The local store was open six days a week. Of course everyone went to church on Sunday, if only to be sociable, and there was usually a Christmas party at the church or the community hall. All in all, it was not a bad life, and though everyone knew everyone else's business, one also had the consolation of knowing that the neighbours were available if anything went wrong.

Life at the resort hotels was a vastly different world. Every summer the urbanites would return by the hundreds, usually aboard the lordly *Sagamo*, to forget about the constraints of city life and resume their carefree holidays, playing golf, tennis, and croquet, or taking up archery, motorboating or fishing. Of course there was always the daily swim at the public beach (shared by all the hotels), and the formality of dressing up for dinner — though activities were far less structured than they had been before the First World War. Windermere House usually had a band from Toronto (or at least a pianist) to entertain its guests at suppertime and in the evenings, when there was often to be a dance. About half the guests were Americans. The Fife House and the Maple Leaf House were smaller and less formal, but sometimes their guests came over to the "grand hotel" to share in the activities or have dinner. Sometimes the local cottagers would also join in (and attend church on Sundays), but neither group tended to interact very much with the villagers, except those who might be employed at the stores and hotels. Those in the latter category tended to get fewer and fewer as the years went by: the hotel generally preferred to hire college students from the cities rather than local young people, partly because the former were usually available to start work sooner, and because they were judged more mature. Indeed, to the villagers, the great hotel, while a vital economic asset, seemed a very exclusive place, filled entirely by the well-to-do; the locals did not feel welcome there. Still, they usually tolerated the annual invasions good-naturedly, knowing that come the fall the community would be theirs again.

Windermere House was still carrying on as usual under Leslie Aitken and his family, with the important difference that the Aitken farm was now gone. Since 1919, when the golf course was started, the hotel relied on foodstuffs mainly from the farm of Charles Roper, who had married Leslie's sister Gertrude. The Aitken farm, which pastured a herd of dairy cattle (plus pigs, which were fed on leftovers from the hotel), was usually run by an English farmer named William Beavan.

The hotel itself required a staff of about fifty to sixty people. The dining room alone required twelve to fifteen waitresses, plus the manager and hostess. Some of the guests, anxious to be first at the golf tees in the mornings, would place their breakfast orders the night before. The kitchen had four or five cooks working under the master chef — not to mention those employed in the salad pantry. There were usually about six housekeepers or chambermaids (mostly local women), three or four groundskeepers, a social director, and about four receptionists in charge of the front desk. Sometimes jobs were rotated. Electric lighting was now provided by a steam-powered generator, while a hot-air engine — later replaced by gasoline-powered pump — brought in the water. At the rear of the hotel was a spice garden, which also produced corn, tomatoes, and flowers; watercress was obtained from the adjacent Baldwin's Creek. Guests amused themselves by playing golf, tennis, or shuffleboard, or they might read, or go swimming. Canoes and sailboats were also available, and one could always take a cruise on the *Sagamo*. Everyone was expected to dress for dinner, although by the 1930s golfing attire was considered sufficient. The staff had fun too, in their own recreation room near the parking lot. Sometimes they would hold their own parties on a local hilltop at night, during the off-hours. Occasionally the boys would play mean tricks on the girls (such as turning their beds upside down), and the girls might retaliate by hosing down the boys' dormitory through a window. But despite such hijinks (or because of them) staff morale was usually quite good.

At any resort hotel, much depends upon the personality of the manager. Leslie Aitken, like his father, was a rather reserved, stern-looking man, very much the perfectionist, and with a strong sense of propriety. Some even considered him a bit of a "stuffed shirt," though occasionally he could surprise people with a little droll humour. He had a special passion for horses and mischieviously named one "Maudie" — to the great annoyance of Maude, his wife. Occasionally, when he knew she was within hearing, he used to vex her by pretending to insult the animal. Mrs. Aitken, a gracious though outspoken lady, made an excellent hostess. For a few seasons Maude and Leslie, along with Gertrude and Charles Roper, spent their winters running another hotel in Florida.

By the summer of 1926 the Fife House, which had been enlarged a little and renamed the Waldorf by Thomas Johnston, was back in the hands of the Fifes, under the old name. Arthur William Fife, the third son of David Junior, repurchased the property from Thomas Huggard, who had acquired it from Johnston three years earlier. It was then showing some of the symptoms of decay, but Arthur, assisted by his wife, Jessie Ray Davidson of Brackenrig, made many alterations and improvements, including the addition of a fine new stone fireplace, and under them the hotel flourished again. It now had thirty-one rooms and could take about sixty-five guests, usually including many children. (Guests at Windermere House were far more likely to send their children off to camp.) Arthur Fife was a lively, cheerful man, very fond of music, and no doubt his personality had much to do with the resort's revival. The Ingleside House, by contrast, was slowly dying with its owner, and in 1925 the Aitkens arranged to purchase it from Mrs. Inglis for three thousand dollars, on the understanding that she could still use it as long as she wished. She died in 1931, and the property was absorbed into Windermere House. The old Ingleside was then torn down and a garage built on the site.

By the end of the 1920s Windermere had become a prosperous and contented little tourist village. It still had unachieved goals and unfinished business, but it was a happy little place, bustling in the summers and quiet in winter. Most villagers, in 1929, would probably have assumed that the future would continue to be like the past.

Aerial view of Windermere House, facing south, with Fife House at top right, ca. 1948. (Edwin Paullette)

• CHAPTER 3 •

THE DIFFICULT YEARS (1930–1970)

OCTOBER 26, 1929, WAS A FATEFUL DAY, even for Windermere. Panic struck the New York Stock Exchange as frightened investors suddenly rushed to sell off scores of overvalued stocks. Despite a few rallies in succeeding weeks, the downward spiral continued, putting hundreds of shaky firms out of business and thousands of people out of work. Debtors defaulted, customer orders dried up, and soon other firms likewise collapsed, or had to cut production and dismiss staff. The shock waves were felt all around the industrialized world. Soon hundreds of thousands of unemployed men were riding the rails all over the country looking for work, increasing the strain on hard-pressed communities trying to feed and house them. Dust bowls in the prairies intensified the misery. The results were hardship, despair, loss of self-esteem, and even suicide, as governments, businessmen, and ordinary citizens struggled with an invisible malaise they could not understand, but which had produced glaring want in the midst of plenty.

Muskoka first noticed the effects in the spring of 1930 when, despite the fine weather, relatively few tourists appeared. By July it was clear that most of the summer people were not coming back, and that the local communities would largely have to fend for themselves. Few parts of Ontario had become so dependent on seasonal visitors, and soon the resorts and the lake steamers became very hard-pressed. Several hotels either closed or burned during the "Dirty Thirties," and those that survived had to cut as many corners as possible. So began the dreary, wasted decade of the Great Depression.

The village of Windermere perhaps suffered less than most. Perhaps its position as the terminus of a road meant that relatively few transients passed through it. Besides, many of its people either had farms, or had relatives who did, which meant that they did not have to starve. Even so, William Aitken was often obliged to extend credit to some of his hard-pressed neighbours for as long as two years. (On one occasion Fred Aitken had to insist that his son Allen, who was making a delivery to a difficult customer at Muskoka Beach Inn near Gravenhurst, should not unload his truck until an old account of six hundred dollars had been settled; Allen was made to wait a long time and to listen to all sorts of excuses, but in the end he got his cheque.) Certainly the times were difficult, and in 1931, the United Church Women sent a large consignment of old clothes to help destitute farmers in Saskatchewan. The village also looked after the children of the unambitious "Richey" Lance, son of Dick, the storekeeper, until Henry Longhurst (with some help from Albert Matthews) arranged to relocate most of the family to a farm near Sutton, Ontario.

Meanwhile, many old landmarks were disappearing, though not always because of hard times. One day, during the summer of 1929, the Clark sawmill went up in flames while the crews were at work, and despite all efforts the plant was soon reduced to a heap of charred ruins. It was never rebuilt, and perhaps sixteen or twenty men lost their jobs. Overheated bearings in the machinery were suspected of causing the blaze.

Other old landmarks soon followed. The Ingleside House, now owned by Windermere House, was demolished by 1931 and a garage built on its site for the hotel vehicles. Shortly afterwards the handsome little Presbyterian church, now surplus, was torn down. In 1932 the Huggard home and store burned down, but were speedily rebuilt.

Also in 1932 the Canadian Chautauqua at Epworth Inn had to shut down: when people are trying to make ends meet, they cannot spend much on culture, and soon the lively, stimulating summer sessions on Tobin Island became a thing of the past. The inn was acquired by George Martin, a Toronto advertising executive who was an expert on promotional activities; it is said that he could make anything pay! Martin renamed the hotel Wigwassan Lodge (silver birches) and kept it running as a large resort hotel for another quarter century. The resort was so popular that some guests took space in the boathouse or even occupied tents for a time. Wigwassan catered mainly to fun-loving young people and acquired a reputation of being a rather noisy place, while its neighbour Windermere House, attracted older folk and remained set in its quiet ways. Even so, Martin remained on good terms with Leslie Aitken. As roads were gradually paved and improved during the 1930s (partly as a form of unemployment relief), more and more tourists began to drive to Muskoka, deserting the trains and the steamboat line, and Martin had to provide a fleet of Ditchburn motor launches to help ferry patrons in from Windermere. It was soon a problem to find parking space for all the cars in the village.

Meanwhile, the Maple Leaf House held its own during the Depression. As of 1933 it had 35 guest rooms, as compared with 50 at King's Park, 31 at the Fife House, and 120 at Windermere House. Irenaeus Hough seemed to get more and more cantankerous in his old age, and after his wife died he hired two sisters from Raymond to work at the hotel; he soon married one, but had children by both!

A glimpse of Mr. Hough's personality has been afforded by John E. Montgomery of Toronto, who, at twenty-three, left Manitoulin Island to work at the Maple Leaf House in 1933. He got off the train at Utterson at two in the morning, expecting Mr. Hough to pick him up, but Hough did not arrive until after daybreak, and the young man had to sleep on a station bench. Montgomery spent two months gardening, splitting wood, planting trees, milking cows, and doing farm work for fifteen dollars a month plus board. Then on July 1, having put in a twelve-hour day, he decided to take a breather and visit the Windermere store, only to be fired on his return because he hadn't been at the gas pumps when a late-night customer arrived! This was a bitter blow, but Montgomery was allowed to stay the night, on condition that he milk the cow as usual the following day. He then left with thirty dollars in his pocket and nowhere to go, but the Fifes, unwilling to see him left without a place to sleep, gave him a job for the next two months at the same wages. On Labour Day a friendly police constable gave him a ride to Stayner, whence he found his way home by boat. Montgomery concluded that there were "nice people in Windermere!"

Rather surprisingly the village was actually gaining in tourist accommodation at this time. In 1932, after Tom Clark Junior died, part of the shoreline property in the bay south of Clark's Falls went to his sister Rachel, who had married Nathaniel Bogart, once the operator of the local marina. Their son Gordon, a general handyman and sawmill owner from Ufford, began developing a small cabin resort at Sunset Bay, facing Wigwassan Lodge. The site had about 900 feet of

WHARF AND MARINA, CA. 1930. PUMPHOUSE AT LEFT.

shoreline and a safe, sandy beach. At the suggestion of an Ojibwa woman, it was named Paquana (originally Pauquana, meaning "sumach"). Bogart built a shed and a log lodge building, and then a series of cottages, known as Sunset, Clearview, and Cosy, plus a staff house with four bedrooms. The three cottages had a total of five bedrooms and could accommodate about eighteen people; meals were served at the lodge. Later, a white house was added to the rear of the lodge, complete with a kitchen and a staff bedroom upstairs. Boat storage facilities were also developed. The venture prospered and had special appeal to families of modest means who could afford to drive to the lakes for a few weeks' holiday. In 1945 the staff house was moved closer to the lake to make way for a stone wall at the edge of the property to support the embankment for a new road to Clark's Falls. The property was put up for sale in 1950 Mrs. Bogart died.

In 1930 William Aitken retired from the mercantile business and handed his store over to his reluctant son, Fred (who was already operating Windermere Transport). Fred carried on with it, assisted by his sister Irene, plus a butcher and one or two clerks in the summertime. In 1935 Arthur Bilz, a carpenter from Sprucedale, opened a second store on the main street, close to the United church, with the encouragement of Henry Longhurst, who did not care to shop at the Aitken store, but this operation did not last long. The community was too small to sustain two stores, and Mr. Bilz ran his in a somewhat haphazard way. Later the Bilz store became the local office of the Watt Municipal Telephone system, whose main switchboard was at Utterson. William Aitken became the chairman of the telephone system, and had to endure much criticism for faulty lines and deteriorating service; as a result, the company had few subscribers. (Around 1958 the Bell Telephone Company would establish itself in a little building close to the corner of the Longhurst Road.)

The village itself continued to make local improvements. It had its school and hockey rink, and presently Reeve Longhurst came up with the idea that it should also form its own hydroelectric company — not to generate its own power, of course, but to buy it wholesale from Ontario Hydro and resell it to local subscribers at the same price. (Until then, only Windermere House itself and the Aitken store had

STORAGE (OIL) BUILDING, STORAGE HOUSE FOR STORE, STORE (PAULLETTE'S), OLD DAIRY (FORMER BARBER SHOP) AT RIGHT, WINDERMERE, CA. 1940S. (FLORENCE AITKEN)

power, which was supplied by a steam generator.) The council approved the proposal, but financing it was a problem; the estimated cost was to be $19,600! A bylaw was passed to authorize the issuing of bonds, to be paid for over a period of twenty years, but there were few takers. The Matthews Company offered seventy-one cents on the dollar for them, and Ontario Hydro accepted them as collateral; afterwards the whole lot was purchased by Hugh Cayley. By 1930 the lines were up and Windermere Hydro was in business. It required only a single paid employee to act as secretary and read the meters, and in the event of problems it could always enlist help from Ontario Hydro (usually Edward Armstrong and William Thompson of Utterson would be sent over to service the lines, free of charge). For about fifty-five years it worked quite nicely.

In 1930 Canadian National Telegraphs opened an office at the Aitken store, and a youthful Edwin Alfred Paullette, who had learned telegraphy at Parry Sound, moved in as the operator. He too, became a permanent resident of the village, rooming with William Aitken. His duties were considerable: the local telephone service was then in poor shape, and there might easily be fifteen hundred telegrams received and sent every summer. Besides, the hotels preferred telegraph messages, which were written and therefore legally binding, while businessmen, such as C. L. Burton of Simpson's, wanted regular reports from Toronto. Gradually Paullette began to take on the postal work as well. The mail was delivered once daily from Utterson during the winters and arrived four times daily during the summers, aboard the *Cherokee* and the *Sagamo*.

Cottage construction continued, mainly in the hands of Henry Longhurst's sons, Milton and Mervin, and their rival, Milton Goltz. There was no love lost between the two camps, and it is rather ironic to note that ultimately Robert Goltz, a grandnephew of Milton, would take over the Longhurst carpentry business. In 1930 Mrs. Margaret Eaton, who was now in failing health, parted with her beloved Ravenscrag and died soon afterwards in Toronto. Gradually all the other Eatons faded from the local scene, and after the Second World War, Ravenscrag was purchased and demolished by Britton Osler Jr. who replaced it with a new cottage. In 1934 Irwin Miller likewise passed away; the Llanllar estate then passed to Miss Elsie Sweeney, one of his in-laws, who became very active in village affairs. She began the practice of allowing the general public in to picnic and admire the famous gardens once a week for a fee; she donated the proceeds to the United church.

AITKEN FAMILY, CA. 1940. (FLORENCE AITKEN)

During the 1930s the local roads were being improved and even paved near the larger towns, and by about 1939 most freight and mail deliveries were being made by truck. Blizzards were still a problem, however, and it was usually the responsibility of Milton Longhurst, the road commissioner, to keep the roads plowed out. He did this by using a heavy, horse-drawn, V-shaped plow built and designed by Gordon Dawson. Mounted on a sleigh, the plow could cut through three-foot drifts, using three teams of horses — two pulling and one pushing! Ed Paullette commonly handled the lead team, with Dawson on the tongue of the plow and Longhurst on the push pole. The rig worked very well, and also cleared the Dawson Road in Watt; later it was supplemented by an army truck.

By about 1939 the government of Mitchell Hepburn passed legislation requiring that all milk sold to the public must be pasteurized.

This meant that a plant was required, and in June of 1940 Fred Aitken and his wife, Florence, concluded that the community needed a dairy. They borrowed five hundred dollars and proceeded to take over the old, vacant Fife store alongside their own, where they installed all the tanks, pumps, coolers, and weigh scales necessary for pasteurization. Knowing nothing about this process, they hired a Kitchener man named Byron Weber to manage the plant, and meanwhile began buying milk from the local farmers. Initially the dairy produced about four hundred quarts of milk every day, but this was soon increased to four thousand quarts during the summers; if this proved insufficient, more could be ordered from Bracebridge. Inspectors appeared every week, and any ill-smelling milk was discarded. Soon Windermere Dairy was distributing bottles of fresh milk to stores, marinas, camps, cottages, and homes all the way from Falkenburg and Brackenrig to Rosseau and even Minett, as well as east to Utterson and Port Sydney. Wilson's Lodge and Camp Winnebago on Skeleton Lake were important customers; the camp alone had six hundred children to feed. Five trucks were required during the summers, and many extra deliveries were necessary. Sometimes Florence would take the wheel as "gopher" if no one else was available. (On occasion she was known to encounter the famous singer Gordon Lightfoot, of Orillia, on the Rostrevor Road.) Island deliveries were made by way of the Wigwassan water-taxis. Sometimes eight or ten people worked for the dairy, at least part-time, including Bernie Beavan and Horace Taylor, who drove the trucks for twenty-five years. The only potential competition came from Walker Riley of Milford Bay, who threatened to put Aitken out of business, though there was no actual competition at all. Besides milk, the dairy also sold purchased butter and ice cream. The business flourished, and by 1966 Mr. Aitken built a whole new building, of concrete blocks, on the Rostrevor Road at the outskirts of the village. The new site was close to some natural springs near the Dee River, which provided plenty of water. When the Ontario government established the Milk Marketing Board, which dictated that the Windermere Dairy must accede to quotas set in distant North Bay (often unrealistically high), and all sorts of other restrictions. Fred felt that the business was no longer his. In 1967 he sold out to Briars, which soon shut down the operation. Many local dairies across Ontario met the same fate. Shortly afterwards, Fred Aitken himself died.

SCENE FROM THE R.M.S. *Sagamo*, CA. 1945. THE TUG *Niska* IS AT THE SIDE DOCK. (MRS. I. W. DICKSON)

In the meantime there had come the grim news of the outbreak of the Second World War, which again resulted in rationing of foods, clothing, and gasoline, and once again the Windermere resorts had to tighten their belts in order to survive. Men also became scarce, as the military situation in Europe deteriorated and more and more were called to the colours. But there was still no prohibition on rail or steamship travel, and by now everyone had a job. Soon the passenger ships were crowded again as people flocked back to the resorts. Charlie Musgrave, the Toronto musician who was then commentator on the *Sagamo*, when announcing the attractions of lovely Windermere, was

R.M.S. *Sagamo* DOCKING AT WINDERMERE. (PAO)

careful to point out that the village had no cemeteries — because it was such a healthy place that no one ever died there!

When the guns and bombs of war finally gave way to victory celebrations in May of 1945, the village went wild with joy, and people turned their attention back to their own lives and community improvements. Within about three years the automotive and boat-building companies were back to peacetime production levels, and soon the lakes were swarming with speedboats. By this time Basil Veitch of Ufford had taken over the marina, running a large motorboat called the *Shirl-evon* as a water-taxi; sometimes he would run hotel guests over to Port Carling for performances by the Straw Hat Players. His wife, Dolly, operated the Rooftop Gardens, a coffee shop and restaurant on the upper floor of the marina, where delicious milkshakes and ice-cream cones were sold. In 1950 Edwin Paullette and his wife, Kay, took over William Aitken's store, and with it the post office.

While motorboats flourished, the lake steamers resumed their leisurely decline. After 1950 only the *Sagamo* and the *Segwun* were still plying the lakes. And while the latter ship continued to drop off the summer mail daily, it was seldom that any of the local people could be induced to take a cruise. The resorts were now more likely to charter Bruce Wallace's big, white motor launch, the *Viola* (usually based in Windermere), for their guests; sometimes she would run all the way to Bala for an evening of dancing at Dunn's Pavilion. The *Sagamo* paid her last visit to Windermere in August of 1958, then left for Gravenhurst, never to return.

Road improvements resumed. By about 1949 roads from Utterson had been paved, or at least oiled, although corduroy roads existed around Ullswater for many years. The Brackenrig Road remained little more than a wagon road until 1960. Once improved, it shortened travel time to Port Carling from forty minutes to fifteen. A result of this has been Windermere's protection by the Port Carling Fire Department. The Aitken Transport service continued all through these years, but in 1970, following Fred Aitken's death, Orvil Hammond, of Bracebridge, who ran his own transport business, bought up the Aitken licences.

Sports flourished. Around 1953 a rifle club was organized by Irving Pettit for target shooting at Paquana. Norman Stripp, who had moved to Windermere around 1946, became its first president and about twenty-four people joined up. Some were experienced hunters from Ufford, Raymond, and Bent River, who purchased very expensive rifles and competed for Dominion Marksmen medals. In later years the club purchased a new property near Ullswater and put up a new building, doing their firing through slits. The group still survives, but today it has barely half a dozen members left. A bowling team, with both men's leagues and a ladies' league, was formed in the 1960s; the actual bowling was done at Bracebridge, where the men's team won the championship one year. Likewise, the Windermere Curling Team was organized to play at Bracebridge; so many joined it that two teams had to be formed. Milton Goltz was the skip. There was still the hockey team, coached by Samuel Stripp, Norman's father, which sometimes competed at Port Carling, in uniform. Local games were played on a rink behind the old Forge house.

Like most communities, Windermere has had its share of fires. Around 1950 the Goltz family garage and workshop near the United church burned early one evening; it was rebuilt. In 1959 the former Clifford Marshall cottage — a huge structure on Maple Leaf Bay close to the Baldwins — went up in a spectacular blaze. Most locals believed it was arson. One evening around midnight — sometime during the mid 1960s — the home of William Bunn, the golf course superintendent, caught fire too. The church bell sounded the alarm but the building was gutted. (It was rebuilt by the golf club.) About that time Osborne Longhurst's winterized cottage likewise burned; it too was rebuilt. Many villagers were secretly apprehensive about the safety of the great hotel itself, fearing that if a blaze ever got started there, it might spread sparks that could consume the entire village. During the 1960s a volunteer fire department was formed. Trucks, a water carrier, two portable pumps, and three or four hoses were obtained and housed at the Windermere House garage; later a Quonset hut was built. Water was drawn from the lake. Charles Roper became the first chief, followed by James Poirier and Eric Parker. After Muskoka Lakes Township was set up, a new hall was built a few miles from the village, and the old Quonset hut was demolished.

LESLIE AITKEN'S AUTOMOBILE, WINDERMERE, CA. 1916. LITTLE IRENE AITKEN (BRIESE) STANDS ON THE RUNNING BOARD. (FLORENCE AITKEN)

By the late 1940s the old United church building was deteriorating and becoming overcrowded, and furthermore, the church women wanted a basement in which to conduct their work. Since the building sat on solid granite, it was clear that a whole new building would have to be built. A number of cottagers, including the Millers and Sweeneys, took the lead in proposing a new church to be built of stone, but several years passed before anything was done. At last financier Harry Gundy of Toronto, who had a cottage north of Rostrevor, declared, "Let's get started before we're all dead!" In 1950 a building committee of seven was formed, chaired by Leslie Aitken and consisting of three cottagers — C. L. Burton, W. G. Whiteside and Dr. O. W. Neimeier — plus Milton Goltz and Ed Paullette. Later Mr. Stanley Grant was added.

It was decided to build on the same site, and to engage Milton Goltz as contractor, with the result that Henry Longhurst refused to have any part in the project, though almost all the other villagers did. (Henry's sons Mervin and Milton did deliver a little gravel for cement, which Goltz rejected because it was full of impurities.) C. L. Burton asked his architect, Frank Corley, to donate his services by designing the new building and also persuaded the Western Canada Lumber Company (of which he was a director) to provide the cedar shingles. Simpson's covered the costs until the following spring.

After Labour Day the old church was closed and demolished; services were transferred to the little Sunday school building. Adrian Hicks dynamited the bedrock for the basement, and the loose stone was used in the new building. Clifford Smith and John Bunn did the external masonry work, while Fred Aitken used his transport truck to bring in the new pews and furniture. Mr. Goltz contributed piped spring water from his nearby home into the basement kitchen. Miss Elsie Sweeney donated the electric organ and also had the grounds landscaped by the gardeners from Llanllar. Countless people helped in the project, which was largely completed by volunteer labour and gifts of materials and furnishings, usually in memory of a departed friend or relative. Nonetheless, funds ran short before the winter ended, and Leslie Aitken, Milton Goltz and Ed Paullette had to advance personal loans to keep things going. The president of a wiring company, who cottaged on Lake Rosseau, agreed to supply all the electrical cables without charge, while donations poured in from cottagers, hotel guests, the Windermere Golf and Country Club, and from Windermere House itself.

MAPLE LEAF LODGE (NOW THE BALDWINS), CA. 1945. (THE BALDWINS)

The church is built of red granite in Gothic style and looks like something transplanted from England. It has stained-glass windows over the altar, with side panels depicting the rocks, trees, and waters of Muskoka, while the rear wall contains a bronze plaque honouring the three founding settlers: Francis Forge, David Fife amd Thomas Aitken, all of whom had been pillars of the original church. It was completed in 1951, but despite all the contributions, the total bill came to about fifty-five thousand dollars. Renewed subscriptions soon took care of the balance. (Tourists and cottagers paid about ninety-one percent of the total.) Today Windermere United Church is an architectural jewel. Many ministers, including several cottagers, have conducted services there, and not surprisingly it has hosted many weddings. Its only serious drawback is that it is expensive to heat, but it is still one of the focal points of the community and is used year round. Every October the United Church Women hold a mammoth Thanksgiving dinner, often cooking up to thirty pies and twenty-eight turkeys to serve as many as six hundred patrons.

The little Anglican church, by contrast, is a summer church, once used mainly by cottagers. A fire destroyed the rectory, and the church itself barely survived the 1960s, but the Osler, Mockridge and Skinner families helped to revive it, and it has also drawn new life from some of the recent arrivals in Windermere. The Reverend Ronald Armstrong, noted for his famous mission on the Caribbean island of Bequia, was long a popular incumbent, until his untimely death in a plane crash in 1992. Relations between the Anglican and United churches have always been friendly, and the Anglicans, when faced with bad weather, have been known to hold their annual strawberry social in the basement of the United church.

Soon after the United church was completed, Reeve Longhurst advocated that the village should have its own municipal hall. He suggested that the old, vacant Sunday school building (the original Methodist church) be acquired and moved across the street to the site of the former Huggard store, but instead, John Bogart, a farmer from Ufford, bought it and demolished it, using the timbers for some cottages he was building on Three Mile Lake. Henry Longhurst persevered with the proposed hall. It was designed by J. K. Partridge, a local cottager, and built of brick, under the direction of Joseph Fullerton, whose family settled originally at Skeleton Bay, Lake Rosseau. The building was paid for by cash subscriptions. In September 1953 it was opened and soon supplied with a fireproof vault. It became the Windermere Community Centre (until the old schoolhouse became available in 1966) and provided a home for the Lions and Seniors' clubs, plus the Women's Institute. Renovated in 1971-72, today it is used mainly for art exhibitions, quilting bees and special shows.

During this period, many of the resorts changed hands. In 1941 the irascible Irenaeus Hough sold the Maple Leaf House to his son Ivan Reginald and retired. Ivan, who had won paddling medals for Canada at the 1924 Olympics, remodelled the hotel and renamed it Maple Leaf Lodge. The main building then had eight rooms on the main floor and ten on the second, with one bathroom on each floor. An annex called the Snuggery had an additional ten rooms. For entertainment the lodge offered a concrete tennis court, horseback riding, baseball, dancing, boating, and swimming, at rates of sixteen to twenty-five dollars per week on the American plan. In May of 1946 Ivan Hough sold Maple Leaf Lodge to Frederick Garnet Baldwin and his wife, Mildred, for fifteen thousand dollars and left to become a chiropractor in Huntsville. Baldwin, a former sports coach at the Ontario Agricultural College at Guelph, had never managed a resort before, but he and his wife gamely took up the challenge; they enlarged and repanelled the hotel, added a snack bar and built several cottages. They also changed the name to the Baldwins, as it is still known today. A whole repertoire of new sports activities were introduced, including badminton, croquet, shuffleboard, horseshoes, archery, and table tennis. Boat cruises and dances at neighbouring resorts were also options. The hotel's home-cooked meals were famous, and honeymooners were "catered to with studied neglect." After dinner was storytelling time, and sometimes the guests held costume parties, at which the men would dress up in their wives' clothing and wear ice buckets as hats, while the women dressed as Polynesians, wearing "grass" skirts made from materials purchased at Port Carling. (The children wore homemade costumes.) The Baldwins had definitely become a fun place to stay.

FRED BALDWIN

Mildred Baldwin died in 1953, but Fred — commonly known as "Baldy" — remarried and carried on. It is said that he used to patrol the place at night with a shotgun and play poker with his buddies in the basement of the snack bar. He died in February 1962, but his widow, Mary, continued by herself for another three years.

Around 1945 Lloyd Smith engaged Mervin and Milton Longhurst to convert the old Newtonia building on Maple Leaf Bay into a small resort, which he named Silver Birches. Silver Birches had about five bedrooms and took perhaps twenty guests, but it did not survive very long, and was soon demolished to make way for a private cottage. In 1945 the Trumps sold Rostrevor Lodge to Charles Linton Stark of York County for twenty-five thousand dollars and left the region. Stark and his wife carried on with it until 1951, catering generally to a less-exclusive clientele, then sold it to Arthur H. Bennett and his wife for forty-five thousand dollars. The Bennetts ran it successfully until 1965, when it went to Donald Dale Dobson of Orillia and his wife, Shirley, for a comfortable $102,157! The Dobsons, too, made a success of it for some time, taking about 120 guests, although not in the lodge itself, on account of the fire risk. The patrons, many of whom were second-generation visitors, slept in the adjacent cabins and came to the lodge for their meals. Few hunted any more; most spent their time boating, fishing, swimming, playing tennis, or golfing at Windermere.

Paquana Lodge also prospered. Around 1941 Irving Pettit, a radio repairman from Hamilton, spent his holidays there with his wife and daughter. Nine years later their son James learned that Paquana was closed and up for sale. He bought it in collaboration with his father, who wanted a change in life. They found it in poor shape: the place hadn't been used in two years, and worse, the tin roof of the boathouse had caved in under the weight of the winter snows. Irving began by winterizing the kitchen building and replacing the boathouse with a new one containing four bedrooms with pot-bellied stoves for warmth. Meals were served, and later the cottages were renovated and enlarged, with private kitchenettes to turn them into housekeeping units. Soon they were able to handle about forty guests. After the first five years, meals were discontinued, thus lifting a heavy constraint on the owners. Guests have come to prefer an unregimented holiday, allowing them to set their own hours and go out to dinner at Windermere House if they like. The lodge was later renovated and its outside pine boards painted white, while two new cabins were built, each with two bedrooms. The resort was now officially known as Paquana Cottages.

VIEW FROM SILVERBIRCHES LODGE. (FLORENCE AITKEN)

King's Park, by contrast, was winding down. Barbara King had run it with difficulty throughout the Depression, sometimes with the help of her friend Mary Shaw. Old-timers still recall the hard-pressed Mrs. Shaw painfully rowing an outboard into the village, while Miss King would be in vain trying to start the motor. When they arrived, Miss King would pick up her mail, write all her replies in the post office, and finally leave — with the unlucky Mrs. Shaw again at the oars! In 1939 Mrs. Gladys Olive Wilson, Barbara's sister, acquired a portion of the resort, which was apparently renamed White Oaks at this time. Miss King soon left for Toronto and died around 1961. In 1946 the White Oaks resort was sold to Mrs. Ellen Meade Armson, who resold it to Gordon and Beverley Heyd of Ottawa in 1962. The Heyds then demolished the hotel and built a large log cottage with numerous bedroom suites on the site. Even so, the name "King's Park" can still be discerned on a huge boulder located near the former steamer wharf.

By the 1960s the resort industry as a whole was in decline. More and more people were deciding that they wanted their own private cottages instead of a few weeks' stay at a hotel, and by 1960 the resorts, which had numbered fifty-seven in 1930, had dwindled to a mere thirty-six. Those around Windermere had no immunity to hardship. Wigwassan Lodge did well as long as George Martin was there to run it, but in 1966 Mr. Martin died and the big hotel virtually died with him. Just two years later, Wigwassan Lodge, grown very shabby, was shut down. The new owners ordered the place demolished and have purposely left the lofty point vacant. Nothing remains of the great hotel today except a solitary gazebo on the slopes, the ruined dock, and the name.

Rostrevor Lodge lasted longer. The Dobsons kept it going until 1973, when they had to sell it to their mortgage trustees, though they seemingly kept the property until 1977. It then went to a firm called Rosseau-Burton Properties and ceased to be a resort. The new owners were interested only in condominium developments, but these proposals created such a furore that they had to be abandoned. The old hotel was then allowed to deteriorate and finally it was demolished. Today the once beautiful property has literally gone to seed: its lawns have turned into hayfields.

The Fife House disappeared even before Rostrevor Lodge. It had continued to flourish as long as Arthur Fife was in charge. He repainted the place, reshingled the roof as required, cut his own grass, and discharged the mortgage. In 1948 he brought his son William Rae Fife in as a partner, but this arrangement did not work well; Bill Fife began to develop an addiction to the bottle. In 1957 Mrs. Fife died, and Arthur no longer had the spirit — or the physical health — to carry on. He died in April 1960, at the age of seventy-three, and was buried at Bracebridge. Bill took over, but was not able to make a success of it. He reputedly spent more time on the golf course than at his desk, and gradually the hotel went to seed. For a time it tended to attract hippie-type guests, who were not a serious nuisance, though they tended to upset some of the rather "uptight" patrons of Windermere House. As business declined, Mr. Fife had to obtain a second mortgage from the Toronto Dominion Bank, among whose directors was the noted industrialist Bruce Matthews, son of Albert, who owned two cottages on Ellen (now Melbourne) Island in Paton Bay. Matthews assumed the mortgage, but it was not paid off. At first the gentlemanly businessman did not press the issue, but finally he lost patience, and when Fife refused to leave he obtained a sheriff's order and took over in 1969. Matthews made no attempt to run the hotel, which was considered

PAQUANA LODGE, CA. 1951. (MRS. JEANNE PETTIT)

something of a firetrap; about 1970 he ordered it demolished. The vacant property was then sold to Windermere House, which proceeded to erect the Settler's Bay winterized condominium units on the site in 1975 — to be rented out to snowmobilers and cross-country skiers. The rest of the property has been groomed like a park.

Windermere House itself was still going strong. Leslie Aitken ran it with success until his death from bone cancer in 1952, leaving it to his only daughter, Mary Elizabeth. Mary Elizabeth, who had practically grown up at the hotel, now made it her whole life. Privately educated at Whitby, she was the consummate businesswoman, always in the forefront making changes. Around 1960 she had the interior of the hotel gutted in order to install larger guest rooms with individual bathrooms in every suite. (Previously there had been bathrooms only at the ends of the halls.) Much of the work was done by Milton Goltz's crews, while Clark and Brown Electrical in Port Carling took care of the wiring. She also built the Terraces, a twelve-unit condominium at the rear of the hotel near the winter office, in 1971, and a concrete water tower, plus the units at Settler's Bay. Around 1963 she bought the marina, but soon reconsidered and sold it to Norman Stripp, a professional mechanic, in 1965. Sometimes she also engaged local musicians, such as Hugh Clairmont of Gravenhurst, Orville Johnson of Bala, and Dr. Gideon Rowntree, an Islington dentist and cottager who could play anything! To her guests she was always the gracious and immaculate hostess; to her staff she was a strict but reasonable boss, always maintaining some aloofness and demanding to be called "Miss Aitken," always the perfectionist but always fair. It is said that when one member of her staff had a row with one of her superiors and was told she was fired, the matter was referred to Mary Elizabeth, who asked the girl

ROSTREVOR LODGE, LAKE ROSSEAU, CA. 1908. (JEAN CATTO COLLECTION)

one question: "Who hired you?" "You did," the girl replied. "And I'll do the firing too!" rejoined Miss Aitken. An avid reader, she also found time to serve on the village council, under Reeve Milton Goltz, and was the first to recommend the practice of zoning. She also arranged an office and surgery at the village hall for Dr. Fennell Archdekin of Port Carling, whom she enticed to act as physician for both the community and the hotel. Only in her later years was she seen to mellow a little, reluctantly agreeing to the installation of a bar at the basement level. She even learned to square dance!

In matters politic, Henry Longhurst served as reeve for several decades, until he finally stepped down in favour of his son Mervin. Afterwards William Skinner took over the job, to be followed again by Henry Longhurst, and finally — to Longhurst's great disgust — Milton Goltz, who held the position until 1970. Henry Longhurst then retired from politics to his home, lived to a great age, and wrote a little book of memoirs. His sons took over the contracting business. Gradually he succumbed to Alzheimer's and spent his last years at the Pines Nursing Home at Bracebridge. He died in 1983, at the age of ninety-nine, and was buried at Ufford. To those who knew him, Longhurst was often considered an autocratic, acquisitive, revengeful man who wanted his own way, disrupted the lives of some of his children, and maintained a bitter and pointless feud with Milton Goltz, which brought him no credit. On the other hand, he was often gracious if properly approached, cofounded the Children's Aid Society of Muskoka, and supported other worthy causes — though he always wanted recognition for his efforts. Certainly he did much for the village of Windermere.

Other amenities developed apace. Around 1964 Lloyd Parker acquired part of the shores of Paton Bay and began the long process of digging out a harbour and filling in land to provide parking and docking facilities for those cottagers who had properties on the neighbouring islands. (Parker's Boat Land is not a marina per se, in that it has no store, boathouses, or gas pumps; boaters continued to call at Windermere Marina for gasoline or motor service.) Today it is run by Lloyd's son Eric and can shelter about one hundred boats. Norman Stripp ran the marina for ten years, including running boat tours, a water-taxi service (using a Ditchburn launch), and a livery with small boats and a pontoon craft, employing two employees and eight extras during the summer; he also sold Imperial Esso gasoline, Johnson outboards and Grew boats. His wife, Harriet, looked after the Rooftop Gardens (now renamed The Skipper) which featured a tea room and gift shop as well as a restaurant. Winters were devoted to renovations. In 1975 Stripp sold the operation to James Burton, a former ski instructor at Wigwassan, and applied himself to repairing boats. Burton shut down the restaurant and largely ceased to service boats unless they were brought to the shop; in addition, the mechanic he hired seemed to have a poor attitude. As a result, business declined. A fire broke out one night in August 1977. It was spotted and put out by Jim Poirier and the fire brigade, but not without some damage to one of the buildings, although fortunately no boats were lost. The following summer Burton sold the business and left. His successor, the Reverend Peter Hill, a cottager from Florence Island and Toronto, had once piloted the launch for Wigwassan Lodge; he still conducts services in the Anglican church every summer. Later, the marina went to James Young, a newcomer from the south, who took it on as a post-retirement job until 1989.

Until 1967 Windermere had no service clubs, although some villagers belonged to the Port Carling Lions Club. Then Norman Stripp and his friend Bill Skinner, a master carpenter who worked for twenty-five years at Wigwassan, decided to establish a branch in Windermere, to serve and improve the community and help those in need. This required at least eighteen charter members, but Stripp and Skinner, aided by Bruce Wallace, managed to line up twenty-two, a few of whom were from Bracebridge. The club meets at the community hall. Its activities have included supporting the CNIB camp on Lake Joseph, Camp Huronda for needy children near Huntsville, school field trips, student exchanges, hospital visits, and seeing-eye dogs. The club has also assisted with rebuilding burned-out homes, and providing crutches and wheelchairs for disabled people. It sponsors a Community Fun Day every July, featuring parades with floats, visits by the Bracebridge Pipe Band, or Wilf Creasor's Hungry Five musicians, swimming and canoe races, three-legged races, a food booth, and fireworks in the evenings. Money is raised through dinners, flea markets, and visits to the sugar bushes in the spring.

In 1970 the Village of Windermere officially ceased to exist.

PAQUANA LODGE BEACH. (MRS. JEANNE PETTIT)

• CHAPTER 4 •

RECENT YEARS (1970–1997)

IN MAY 1970 THE LITTLE COMMUNITY received the official word. The Ontario government of William Grenville Davis was proceeding with the Muskoka Act, which erased all of the existing municipalities (except for the towns of Gravenhurst, Bracebridge, and Huntsville), and reduced them to six consolidated segments, all in the name of greater efficiency and economy. Windermere Village was to be swallowed up in the new Township of Muskoka Lakes, which also included the old townships of Cardwell, Watt, and Medora. The village would not even be granted its own representative on the new township council; it was now part of Ward B.

The villagers were outraged. They had been conducting their own affairs quite nicely and had always been able to balance their budgets and pay for their own expenditures, without extensive taxation. They knew the people running the village council (none of whom were paid) and who to call if there was a problem of any sort. Their roads and hydro lines were in good shape. Now control was being removed from their hands and moved to distant centres like Port Carling and Bracebridge. They protested vehemently, and sent petitions to Queen's Park — in vain. The government was convinced that Muskoka's political institutions needed an overhaul and pushed the Act through despite the objections. The villagers then turned to their churches and community hall, using them as substitutes for local government.

For a time Milton Goltz, the last reeve of the Village of Windermere, became a councillor for Watt on the new Township of Muskoka Lakes Council, until his retirement in the fall of 1972. He died shortly afterwards and was succeeded by Mervin Longhurst, and later by John Young, a newcomer from Oxford County whose wife had a cottage at Windermere. The township has shown a lot of sympathy for the sentiments of the small communities. It has permitted them to retain their community centres and firehalls, and indeed has built a new fire station to serve Windermere and vicinity, close to the junction of Windermere and Dee Bank Roads. It also took over the community hall and the old village school, which became the new community hall and seniors' centre. Windermere children must now attend the new Watt Public School at Ullswater.

Life carried on. In 1974 Florence Aitken came up with the idea of establishing a local library in Windermere. It was formed as a branch of the Muskoka Lakes Library, whose headquarters was at Port Carling. The library at Windermere contained about three hundred books, most from the Algonquin Library Company, which supplied all of the local libraries in Muskoka. Mrs. Kathleen "Kay" Paullette, wife of Edwin, acted as librarian, while a small annual grant paid her salary. The facility, housed in the store, was used mostly by tourists. It survived until 1984. (The big hotels, meanwhile, had small libraries of their own.)

Edwin Paullette had taken over Fred Aitken's store in 1949, though not with great enthusiasm. He removed the gas pumps, which were in the way of operations, and demolished the vacant former dairy building alongside. Business declined gradually. As automobiles became more common, people found that they preferred to shop at Bracebridge, where the selection was much greater, and furthermore, in 1962 Murray Taylor, a nephew of Horace, was persuaded to open a rival store further up the street. He intended it mainly as a meat marketeria and learned the butcher's trade in Toronto, but by stages the business expanded into a general grocery store. His wife, Heather, did much of the actual work of running it, and in 1978 she also became the postmistress, after Ed Paullette and his wife, who were growing old, were required to step down. After Heather died in 1980, Taylor took over the job. Around 1980 a fire broke out in the upper storey of the Taylor store, perhaps as a result of defective wiring. The Port Carling Fire Brigade rushed to the scene and hosed everything down, but that evening the blaze reignited and the trucks had to rush back for a second time to keep the fire from spreading. The Taylors moved temporarily to the old Supertest station across the road until their new, larger, concrete-block building was ready. It continues to serve the village today.

In 1984 Ed Paullette decided to retire and shut down his store. One of the consequences of this was the end of the village library, which was no longer flourishing, despite his wife's previous efforts. The books acquired from the Port Carling Library were returned, while the rest found a new home in the community centre, formerly the village schoolhouse. The store was acquired by the new owners of Windermere House, along with an adjacent house, the old parsonage, and the former Fred Aitken house, which had originally belonged to Francis Forge. These moves aroused considerable apprehension amongst the villagers, who suspected that the owners of Windermere House were planning to gut the core of the community to build condominiums. There was also a proposal to build six retirement homes on a twenty-acre site at Paton Bay. None of these plans were ever carried out. The parsonage is now used by the hotel staff, while the old Aitken store is being sold off to a team of architects from Toronto, who are currently renovating it as a residence and show room.

CLARK'S POND (LAKE PAUQUANA). (MRS. JEANNE PETTIT)

Another loss in village autonomy was the closing of Windermere Hydro. The tiny company had served the community well for about fifty-five years, but Ontario Hydro had begun charging for repairs and maintenance of its lines. Around 1985 Windermere Hydro was sold to the provincial utility.

In 1975 a new enterprise to promote the name of Windermere was founded, though not in the village proper. This was the Windermere Garden Centre, located a little north of Dee Bank. The owners, Marshall and Joan Emmons, are veteran nursery people from Welland who finally decided to move closer to their cottage near Gravenhurst. Mr. Emmons served as gardener for two seasons at Windermere House before establishing his nursery, which has since expanded to become the largest in the area. The firm now employs about twenty-five people; lately, Rick Emmons has taken over the business from his parents. The nursery is also home to several peacocks.

During the 1970s the Windermere seniors helped organize a club known as Win-Dee-Ford, after the three communities it served: Windermere, Dee Bank, and Ufford. The club had about thirty members and was once very active, organizing weekly euchre parties and potluck suppers at the community centre. It also fraternized with the club at Port Sydney-Utterson, and conducted bus trips to such places as the Sudbury Science Centre, the Elmira Maple Syrup Festival, and the like. In recent years the club has declined with the passing of many of its members.

On June 21, 1981, there occurred a rather startling development in Windermere, which really seemed like a return to bygone times. In the distance people thought they could hear a steamboat's whistle. Then, around one o'clock, a large white passenger ship appeared on the southern horizon and glided up to Windermere wharf, seeking permission to dock. She was the *Segwun*. She had just completed her sea trials after an eleven-year refit at Gravenhurst and was now conducting her first cruise to Lake Rosseau in twenty-two years. The villagers could hardly believe their eyes. Many crowded to welcome her — though some considered her an expensive, outmoded denizen of a bygone era and predicted that she would soon revert to a static museum piece. But the veteran vessel refuted the experts and sailed into solvency by 1985. Until 1996 she made regular calls at Windermere, usually on Thursdays, discharging her Gravenhurst passengers for lunch at the hotel, and taking guests from Windermere House and the Baldwins on two-hour sightseeing cruises around Tobin Island. She complements the grand hotel perfectly, and is almost as old.

By 1970 the only tourist facilities left in the village were the two hotels — Windermere House and the Baldwins — plus Paquana and Hillcrest Cottages. Paquana is doing very well. In 1975 Jim Pettit, son of Irving, sold his home and business in Burlington and took over. Aided by his wife, Jeanne, and their son John, they gave the place a new look by putting siding on the buildings and renovating the interiors with new windows, ceilings, and washrooms. In 1978 Fowler Construction of Bracebridge paved the road to the chalets and put in two tennis courts. The following year the Pettits had some bad luck: the boathouse collapsed during repairs following a fall storm, but luckily no one was hurt. A new boathouse was then built over the winter, with three bedrooms upstairs, and at the same time Cosy Cottage was demolished and replaced by a honeymoon suite. Several additional cottages, known as Tamarack, Wigwassan and the Beaver Apartments, have been added since, along with swings, and a sandbox. Starting around 1987 grain has been put out on the lake in the winters to feed the local deer, much to the delight of the guests, while in the summer, feeders are set out for hummingbirds. Jeanne knows all the local birdsongs. Around 1992 the family also adopted an orphaned mallard duck, which became a mascot at the resort. Paquana Cottages now has thirteen cabins, plus canoes, an albacore sailboat, three windsurfers, two rowboats, four fibreglass fishing boats with motors, and five runabouts. The grandchildren of some of the old guests still return to "their" cottages every year.

The Baldwins remained in the hands of Mrs. Mary Baldwin until 1964, when she sold it to Mrs. Ruth Irene Paget, an enthusiastic golfer who had had a lot of experience in the resort business. Mrs. Paget added an outdoor pool, renovated the third floor of the main lodge, combining several small rooms into three larger suites, and also built a new two-storey annex called the Pines near the pool; the Pines contained six more units. For a few seasons she also tried operating her resort year-round, but soon found it too much. Early in the 1970s she enlarged the dining room, and also obtained a liquor licence: brown-bagging was no longer necessary! The bar area became the Red Coach Lounge. Three people staffed the kitchen, along with four or five waitresses and two or three groundskeepers.

In March 1980 Mrs. Paget sold the business to Albert and Patricia Poutanen of Windsor. Al had just spent twenty years working in the chemical industry, while Pat had been engaged in real estate; both were ready for something new. Neither knew much about the resort business, but they set to work heroically in an effort to clean up and remodel the kitchen and the upper balcony of the main lodge in time for the May opening. The Poutanens are avid skiers, and naturally they turned the Baldwins back into a winter resort as well. They groomed the ski trails, built a skating rink, and began to offer bobsledding, snowshoeing, tobogganning, and ice fishing. Of course Santa always comes on December 25!

Not a year passes without some change or improvement at the Baldwins. With the aid of their children, the Poutanens have renovated or improved almost every aspect of the establishment. Outside, their son Michael laid out a nine-hole mini-putt range; inside, a whirlpool, sauna and indoor swimming pool have been added. In 1988-89 the old decaying Snuggery building was bulldozed and replaced by a new office complex, crowned by a turret on one corner, and appropriately named the Maple Leaf House, thus paying tribute to the origins of the resort.

At Windermere House — now one of the few remaining grand hotels dating from the nineteenth century — the Aitken era finally came to an end in 1981. Mary Elizabeth Aitken had been trying continuously to upgrade the great hotel and keep abreast of modern demands. During the 1970s she had added a swimming pool at the front patio for guests who no longer wished to sully their feet with sand at the beach. In 1971 she built ten townhouse-type units known as the Terraces on the former site of the hotel vegetable gardens and the Settler's Bay units in 1975; all are self-contained and have their own kitchenettes. She also obtained a licence for spring and fall conventions. The older guests, however, were dying off, and the younger set wanted such things as movies, pubs, and modern music; in short, they wanted action. Miss Aitken relented a bit in her later years and added a romantic bar to the basement, but finally she grew weary of trying to reconcile old-fashioned dignity with modern tastes, and in 1981 sold the great hotel to George Ember of Toronto, who made a good impression on her. Miss Aitken remained for one more season as an advise. She then withdrew, bought a cottage and did some travelling. She became ill with cancer and died at her home on April 10, 1987, and was laid to rest with her family at Ufford Cemetery.

Windermere House was not the same without her. George Ember seemingly could not handle the myriad details of running such an enterprise, including the budget; maintenance alone cost about a hundred thousand dollars a year. Some of the new patrons were loud and disrespectful, and did not get along well with the older guests. Cindy Dubois, who had risen to the position of hostess under Mary Elizabeth, left in disgust and took up a position at the Chateau Lake Louise. In 1985 Mr. Ember went bankrupt, and the hotel went to a corporation known as Ontario Resorts Inc., part of the Granite Group of companies based in Toronto, which had already taken over several other hotels, including Lakeside Lodge and Paignton House on Lake Rosseau and the Edenvale Inn at Port Carling. The Granite Group sold shares to the public and obtained a large government grant, using part of it to infuse about one million dollars into the great hotel and give it a massive refit. The roof was renewed, the wiring replaced and many structural repairs completed. They also hired a professional manager, Mr. Paul Graham, to run it, and for a time things improved. Graham was loved by the guests, but the Granite Group was dominated by lawyers from the city who knew little about the resort business: some of them wanted to cut costs, by eliminating some of the services guests had come to expect. Besides that, many associates of the Granite Group got into the habit of arriving in the middle of the season, demanding free food and lodgings (even when the dining room was crowded), and generally throwing their weight around. Mr. Graham helplessly endured all this for about three years, then resigned. None of those who succeeded him stayed long.

In the end the Granite Group overextended itself, spent too much money, and began to crumble. One by one, it relinquished the seven hotels it controlled, and soon went out of business. As of 1992 Windermere House was abandoned to its creditors, who decided that the best thing to do was to keep the tottering enterprise going until they could sell it: better to make some money than none. They carried on for three more seasons, but spent the bare mimimum. The public, aware that the great hotel was in receivership, proved skittish about making bookings.

By the fall of 1994 the receivers were about ready to give up and shut the hotel down. At this point, however, a small group of business people, cottagers and former guests decided to take action. They

THE BALDWINS. (THATCHER STUDIO, BRACEBRIDGE)

formed the Windermere Company Limited, which bought the hotel (and the marina) with the intention of keeping them open. They also gave the hotel an extensive refit, including a new roof and decks and a complete repainting. So tasteful and authentic were the renovations that Windermere House received a heritage award in 1995. The season went fairly well, and it looked as if the hotel was winning back the patronage it had lost over the previous years. Then on February 27, 1996, tragedy struck.

Windermere House had been shut down for the winter — as usual — but the management had accepted a proposal from the New Line Cinema Company of Los Angeles to use the hotel for a number of scenes in an action film titled *The Long Kiss Goodnight*, which depicts terrorists attacking a resort during the winter months. (This was in marked contrast to the innocuous *Anne of Green Gables*, which also featured scenes shot at Windermere.) The script called for fires (to be shot off-site using models), but the film company seemed very professional and promised to provide around-the-clock fire protection for the duration. The operation was expected to pump a lot of money into both the hotel and the Muskoka region generally. Almost all the hotel and motel space between Orillia and Huntsville was requisitioned by the film crews, who had made extensive preparations for their shoots — including building a new dummy tower, placed on the roof of Windermere House over the dining room area. On the fateful night, the technicians set up some of their cameras and high-intensity lighting in an upstairs bedroom, close to the north tower. Around eleven o'clock they were ready to begin shooting some night scenes in front of the hotel.

Just minutes later, the word got out that there was a fire in the hotel. At first this was assumed to be a hoax, but shortly afterwards flames could be seen along the peak of the roof, above the room where the technicians had been at work. The alarm was raised, and within minutes the Windermere fire brigade was in action. They were soon joined by the Port Carling brigade, which rushed to the scene in just fifteen minutes. But it was already clear that nothing could save Windermere House. The fire was in the attic, where it could not be reached, and there were no partitions to slow it down. The old, dry hemlock structure provided perfect combustibles, and the conflagration spread rapidly along the roof of the main building, while gradually working its destructive way down. Local citizens tried cutting holes in the ice on Lake Rosseau to accommodate the hoses, but this took too long and the film crews objected, fearing that people might fall in; meanwhile the fire trucks vainly turned a few feeble jets of water on the massive inferno. By now the Bracebridge and Huntsville brigades had arrived, but a hundred trucks and hoses would have made little difference by that point, and the main thing the firefighters could do was make sure the blaze did not spread. (Mercifully, the winds were calm that night.) It might have been possible to salvage things from the main floor, but the firemen refused to allow anyone to try. The fire devoured the main building and spread to the back wing.

Hundreds of people watched the awesome spectacle, many with tears in their eyes. By five in the morning, it was largely over, though the remains continued to smoulder for a long time. Except for the stonework and a spindly, gaunt chimney, nothing remained of the great hotel except a few charred timbers, some twisted metal pipes and appliances, and ashes.

Word of the calamity spread rapidly. It was featured on CBC Television, along with videotaped footage shot by an onlooker, and soon messages of sorrow and condolence poured in, not only from Canada, but also from afar; one such letter arrived from Seoul, Korea. Newspapers in Florida carried headlines about it. The villagers, many of whom seldom went inside the old hotel, still felt devastated and bereaved. Outsiders wondered what would happen to Windermere now that its greatest landmark was gone. (It is said that aviators who had long used the hotel as a guide point on their way to North Bay sometimes got lost once the hotel was destroyed.) The following Sunday an unusual memorial service was held at Windermere United Church. The church was packed to overflowing. Many tributes reached the press, but perhaps the most moving farewell was penned by Mrs. Susan Goltz, who noted that the old hotel had at least departed with dignity. The embarrassed film company announced that it was offering a gift of ten thousand dollars to the Windermere Lions Club, meanwhile it hurriedly made arrangements to depart and finish shooting at Pals of Muskoka (the former Milford Manor Resort). This time there was no fire. For a whole week Mr. William Wakefield, President of the Windermere Company, could not bring himself to walk over and survey the ruins.

The owners did not know what to do next. Some of them wanted simply to collect the considerable insurance money and walk away, leaving the site vacant, but they were already being overwhelmed with hundreds of consolatory messages and letters, most begging them to rebuild. Appeals poured in from the Muskoka Resort Owners Association, the Township of Muskoka Lakes, the Muskoka District, and the Ontario Ministry of Tourism — not to mention the Village of Windermere — all of which promised whatever assistance and co-operation was necessary. Politicians offered to smooth over any difficulties involving the various levels of government, and they were as good as their word: two in particular, Mayor John Young of Muskoka Lakes Township and Councillor Susan Pryke, were staunch supporters and gave much of their time to help. Government bureaucrats came, not to create problems but to help solve them. They even permitted sequential tendering! Even the insurance company supported the reconstruction. Everyone, it seemed, wanted to help.

Finally, in March 1996 the owners announced that they would indeed rebuild Windermere House, in much the same style as before, provided that the insurance proceeds and claims against the movie company would cover the costs. The site was gradually cleaned up and a few relics salvaged, including the silverware and some old liquor bottles which had survived because they had been stored in an old cellar. Architect Joseph Sibbald, of the firm of Victor J. Heinrichs of Toronto, was selected to prepare the plans, and a call to the public went out for any pictures or information about the original building. James E. Twiss, a lawyer from Pickering and now a shareholder in the enterprise, looked after the legal problems. Nonetheless, by the end of May the fire marshal's office had yet to release its official report, and the insurance companies could not yet specify how much insurance proceeds would be forthcoming. Still, a decision on rebuilding could not be delayed if the hotel was to be ready on time for the 1997 season, and when the crucial vote was taken, only one shareholder voted against the reconstruction.

THE REAR OF THE HOTEL, 1988. THE HOUSE IS THE HOME OF GERTRUDE ROPER. (FLORENCE AITKEN)

TRAGEDY AT WINDERMERE, FEBRUARY 27, 1996.

(BRACEBRIDGE *Examiner*)

By the summer of 1996 the plans were ready, and while it proved impossible to salvage the chimney at the south end, all of the old stonework was saved and incorporated into the new building. Some dynamiting was done to prepare a basement for the hotel and to allow space for some new refinements, such as an in-house laundry and an electric elevator. (In the original hotel there had been only a dumbwaiter under the front stairs for hoisting luggage, while the laundry had always been done in a separate building at the rear.) The management also decided to rebuild the septic and drainage fields as well, and to install a fire hydrant, which also protects the core of the village. The lower floors were framed with steel and rebuilt out of Hardyboard, a concrete and cellulose fibre product made to look and feel like wood, while the new dining room windows were custom made to be exact replicas of the originals. (The insurance consultants had suggested steel siding for the exterior walls, but this idea was resoundingly rejected: the company did not want to turn Windermere House into a gigantic garden shed!) The upper storeys have wood frame construction and are amply supplied with sprinkler heads; the pool serves as a reservoir. Heat and smoke alarms abound. At first progress seemed discouragingly slow, but on December 18 the two new prefabricated towers were hoisted onto the roof using a crane. The building was at last enclosed.

Work continued throughout the winter and into the spring. John Andreoli, who had supervised the refit of 1995, was the construction manager, directing about 155 workmen. One contractor, Barnabbas "Barney" Bogart of Bracebridge, worked almost nonstop to get everything ready on time for the projected opening in May, and most of the tradesmen copied his example. The workmen usually had their meals at the Taylor store, which accordingly did a very good business for the duration! Meanwhile new furnishings had been ordered — some of them crafted exactly like the originals — and private groups and citizens offered replica furniture items and pictures to embellish the place. One local resident voluntarily returned the andirons from the old hotel fireplace, which he had scavenged from the ruins. Everyone, it seemed, wanted to see Windermere House back. Even so, it was nip and tuck whether all would be completed on schedule. But done it was, except for parts of the staff quarters on the upper floors. On June 6, 1997, Windermere House was officially reopened. Premier Michael Harris of Ontario, and Bill Grimmett, the MPP for Muskoka, were both in attendance, making short speeches before a crowd of at least three hundred spectators, after which the doors were formally thrown open to the public. A time capsule, containing various old relics and milled from a window frame that had survived the fire, was put on display, commemorating the hotel's first 126 years. It is to be opened in 2123 — 126 years from the opening of the new hotel!

The new hotel differs in some details from the old. It is about three feet wider on the back side and is air-conditioned. The main floor now has several large conference rooms, replacing some private suites in the old, plus a wider hall corridor. French doors open onto the decks and verandahs. The main staircase now descends to the basement, where the bar has been expanded to increase the restaurant space. The upper-floor suites are considerably larger than the originals (some total twelve hundred square feet) and tend to resemble rooms in any modern big-city hotel. The roofline is about a foot higher, and the dormers across the front are positioned a little differently. Balconies have been added to two rooms on the third floor to replace the wooden fire escapes that were part of the original structure. On the other hand, the office, front lounge, gift shop, main sitting room, and the dining room still look almost exactly as they did, despite some consultants' recommendations that the front desk and main lobby be reoriented away from the lake, towards the parking lot — which would have compromised the character of the place completely. Hundreds of old square-headed nails from the original building were reincorporated into the new to strengthen the links with the past. In short, the new hotel, on its ground and basement floors, still feels like the old Windermere House. As Bill Wakefield put it, "Everything has changed — and nothing has changed!" Such a close duplication is almost unprecedented in the history of tourism. The Aitken family would have been pleased.

The new hotel is off to an excellent start. Most of the rooms were fully booked before the 1997 season started, and it successfully won back many former patrons who had drifted away to other hotels. The enthusiasm of the staff, chefs, and management is obvious. Mr. Wakefield, who had to take on the responsibility of becoming the manager — a role he had never assumed before — now looks to the revived resort as his supreme life work. And well may he take pride in his achievement. He has also opened the doors to the community as never before: villagers and the public alike are being urged to come in anytime, have tea, visit the bar, or have dinner. The executive chef, Glen O'Rourke, caters to weddings and conventions, and sometimes has to serve twelve hundred meals in a day; he also teaches culinary classes. Arts and crafts exhibitions have been held here, and in 1997 the National Academy Orchestra, sponsored by ONTV, gave free summer concerts, one on the front lawn. If this trend continues, Windermere House may become a cultural as well as a recreational centre. It also enjoys friendly relations with the Baldwins, which caters to a different sort of clientele, many of whom are seniors. More than ever before, the Grand Old Lady of Lake Rosseau has joined the village community.

Windermere House today has fifty-eight bedroom suites (seventy-seven including the cottage and townhouse units) and can take about two hundred guests. It requires a staff of nearly one hundred to run it, of whom about half live on-site. Meals in the dining room are ordinarily served twice a day, since many guests like to use the hotel as a base of operations for exploring the attractions of the area; however, lunches and dinners can always be obtained at the pub, which has its own kitchen. It is to be hoped that the *Segwun* — which shifted her upper lakes destination to Pinelands Resort during the summer of 1996 — will be able to resume making calls at Windermere. She conducted her Thanksgiving Cruise there in 1996.

The great tragedy has given way to a minor miracle.

• CHAPTER 5 •

CONCLUSION

DESPITE ALL THAT HAS HAPPENED HERE, the Village of Windermere is still a quiet, friendly, little place. There is little likelihood that it will grow much larger in the years to come; space for new housing developments is extremely limited. Nonetheless, many people, tired of the daily rat race of everyday life in larger places, envy its laid-back atmosphere. The village has grown slightly in population lately, though it is hard to obtain a home here. Despite this, a number of younger families have moved in with their children and generally rejuvenated the place. In addition, many cottages have been winterized, though few of their owners stay year-round. Ironically, the village today (1998) has no entry sign; it was removed years ago during highway construction and never replaced.

Even so, the community is extremely busy, hosting art shows, special events, the Lions flea market, and a Fun Day, complete with barbeques and fireworks. It is now home to four bed-and-breakfast establishments: the Top House Retreat (once the home of Henry Longhurst), which is run in a parklike setting by John and Barbara Dutton; the Rowntree Cottage on Dawson Road; Twisted Acres, located close to the Top House; and Dream Catchers, which belongs to the Yieldings on the Brackenrig Road. (Port Carling, a much busier place than Windermere, has no B & Bs at all.)

The Taylor store has been doing very well of late under the direction of Murray and Carol. The Windermere Marina can dock only about fifteen water craft, but there are plans to expand. The ice-cream shop above the marina has been turned into a real-estate office. The United church is less busy than it used to be, but the tiny Anglican church is still well attended. The two support one another's events, and the Women's Institute is now practically shared between the two.

The new Windermere House is a splendid re-creation of the old. While still a very dignified place, the atmosphere there has become far more fluid and relaxed than it ever was under Miss Aitken. It is engaging with the community more than ever before, welcoming villagers to the pub and dining room. It has also become actively involved in community events, and its whole demeanour is much friendlier than it used to be; something the villagers seem to appreciate. There is still an Aitken family presence at Windermere: Allen Aitken, who now runs a trucking business at Huntsville, still owns thirty-two acres of the original family Free Grant. He is the son of Frederick Aitken Senior (the trucker and dairyman), who was the son of William, the storekeeper, who was the son of Thomas, the original settler and founder of Windermere House. Allen's granddaughter Erin still visits regularly, thus representing the sixth generation!

The history of Windermere and its hotels is like a microcosmic sample of the history of Muskoka as a whole. From Ojibwa hunting ground to pioneer settlement to lovely resort area, this small corner has been a vital part of the lives of countless people, including poets, artists, clergy, businessmen and politicians. The very existence of the village of Windermere and its hotels is an inspiration to thousands of people, and helps make Muskoka — and Canada — a better place. Long may they continue to do so!

BIBLIOGRAPHY

PRIMARY SOURCES

ATLASES

Guide Book and Atlas of Muskoka and Parry Sound Districts (edited by W.E. Hamilton, Toronto, 1879)

DIRECTORIES

County of Simcoe Directory and Gazeteer for the Years 1884-5-6 (fourth edition), Hamilton, 1886

Lavell's Business and Professional Directory of the Province of Ontario from 1882. Montreal, 1882

The Union Publishing Company's Farmers and Business Directory for the Counties of Durham, Haliburton, Northumberland, Peterborough and Victoria — and Districts of Muskoka, Nipissing, Parry Sound, Algoma, Rainy River and Thunder Bay, for 1899 (Volume XI) Ingersoll, 1899

GOVERNMENT REPORTS

Department of Railways and Canals: Shipping Registries (Toronto)

District of Muskoka: Land Patent Books, Watt Township

Ontario Legislative Assembly: Sessional Papers; Petitions

Village of Windermere: Minute Books (Community Hall Board)

MANUSCRIPTS

Anonymous: Christ Church (Anglican-Episcopal), Windermere, Ontario

Aitken, Florence: History of Windermere United Church to 1978

Dutton, John & Barbara: Historical Files

Fife, Matthew James: Down Memory's Lane, 1967

Penson, Seymour Richard George: Memoirs (n.d.)

Pettit, Jeanne: Paquana Notes (n.d.)

Poutanen, Patricia: History Books (The Baldwins), Volumes I - IV

Rae, Evelyn Fife: The Fifes of Windermere, Muskoka 1976?

Ullswater Women's Institute: Historical Files

United Church Committee: Windermere United Church Charge: Serving Muskoka for One Hundred Years 1975

Windermere House: Scrapbooks

Windermere Women's Institute: History of Windermere

Wolfe, Dr. Roy I: Recreational Land Use in Ontario (Ph.D. Thesis)

NEWSPAPERS

Bracebridge Examiner

Bracebridge Herald

Bracebridge Herald-Gazette

Bracebridge: Muskoka Advance

Bracebridge: Muskokan

Bracebridge: Muskoka Sun

Bracebridge: Weekender

Toronto Daily Star

Toronto World

PERIODICALS AND BROCHURES

Hotel Accommodation in Ontario, 1933

Muskoka Lakes and Georgian Bay (C.P.R. brochure), ca. 1907

Muskoka Lakes: Highlands of Ontario (brochures), 1903, 1904, 1906, 1909, 1916, 1919

Muskoka Lakes Navigation Company (brochure), 1932

The Muskoka Times & Canadian Tourist Gazette, 1901

Windermere House — Lake Rosseau, Muskoka, Ontario, Canada 1969

SECONDARY SOURCES

Boyer, Barbaranne: *Muskoka's Grand Hotels*, Erin, 1986

Boyer, Robert J: *A Good Town Grew Here in Bracebridge*, Bracebridge, 1978

Cumberland, F. Barlow: *The Northern Lakes of Canada, the Niagara River & Toronto, the Lakes of Muskoka, Lake Nipissing, Georgian Bay, Great Manitoulin Channel, Mackinaw, Sault Ste. Marie, Lake Superior* (Second edition), Toronto, 1886

Deniss, Gary: *A Brief History of the Churches in Muskoka*, Bracebridge, 1997

Deniss, Gary: *A Brief History of the Schools of Muskoka*, Bracebridge, 1972

Du Vernet, Sylvia: *Muskoka Assembly of the Canadian Chautauqua Institution: Points of View and Personalities*, Bracebridge (n.d.)

Fraser, Captain Levi R: *History of Muskoka*, Bracebridge, 1946

Longhurst, Henry: *Reminiscences of Henry Longhurst*, Gravenhurst, 1971

Mason, D.H.C: *Muskoka: the First Islanders*, Bracebridge, 1957

Shea, William Albert: *The History of the Sheas and Birth of a Township*, Peterborough, 1966

Shea, William Albert: *The History of the Sheas and the Paths of Adventure*, Utterson, 1974

Summer Times (anthology), Erin, 1974

Tatley, Richard: *The Steamboat Era in the Muskokas*, Volumes I & II, Erin, 1983, 1984

The author is also greatly indebted to the Municipal Office, Township of Muskoka Lakes, and the Windermere Women's Institute, for freely sharing maps, pictures, and record books about Windermere and its environs. He also owes an enormous debt to many private persons, most especially Mrs. Florence E. Aitken and Mr. Edwin A. Paullette, who not only supplied countless photographs and endured a dozen interviews, but also very kindly reviewed the text and recommended a great many beneficial changes and corrections. Many other past and present residents of Windermere and Watt have also furnished invaluable information at various times, including the late Miss Mary Elizabeth Aitken, Mr. Robert Allsopp, Mr. Myron Beathune, Mr. Jeff Brown, Mr. Aubrey Bogart, Mrs. Cynthia DuBois, Mr. and Mrs. John Dutton, Mr. James Arthur Fife, Mr. William Rae Fife, Mrs. Susan Goltz, Mr. and Mrs. Donald Elmer Klingbeil, Mr. and Mrs. Jack Klooster, Miss Evelyn Longhurst, Mr. Henry Longhurst, Ms. Katherine Nasmith, Mr. Eric Parker, Mrs. Jeanne Pettit, Mrs. Patricia Poutanen, Mr. William Skinner, Mrs. Edith Smith, Mr. Norman Stripp, Mr. James Twiss, and Mr. William Wakefield.

Finally, the author wishes to salute the owners of Windermere House, most notably Mr. James Twiss and Mr. Wakefield, for demonstrating the courage and foresight necessary to rebuild the beautiful "Lady of the Lake" in its original style and elegance after the tragedy of February 27, 1996. They have tastefully restored one of Lake Rosseau's loveliest landmarks, and an essential component of the Muskoka scene, and may also have saved the village of Windermere itself from oblivion. By way of formal dedication, the book is theirs.

LEFT: METHODIST CHURCH, WINDERMERE. (EDWIN PAULLETTE) RIGHT: WIGWASIN LODGE, TOBIN ISLAND. (FLORENCE AITKEN)

S.S. *Edith May*, CA. 1898.

AT ECHO ROCK, LAKE JOSEPH. (MICKLETHWAITE, NATIONAL ARCHIVES OF CANADA PA163292)